Father loves you Alex

From another hunter & fisherman

M. James Jordan

At Home in the Hills

The Tracks of a New Zealand hunter

By M. James Jordan

Dedicated to Dennys, Robin and Ross Smith.
Lifelong mates.

Mountain Lore

When you go into the hills
May the mountains become your friends.
May their companionship and the views they give
Expand not only your lungs,
But also your heart to greatness.

As the shade in the valleys defines it's secrets,
May your time there give you true knowledge of yourself
And humility to your soul.

May your path ever lead to your dreams,
Your legs always leap to the hill,
And your breath be steady and slow.

May the trees be your home,
The rivers and streams your playmates,
And the sky your wise counsellor.

May your camp have an abundance of dry wood,
Your stomach be filled at each meal,
And strangers add warmth to your fire.

When the summer days bring peace to your heart
May it return in the solitary nights
When sleep is hard to find.

When loneliness assails, may you find new challenge.
When exhaustion creeps up, may you find warm shelter.
When snow smothers movement, may you have ample supplies.
When winds howl, may your bed be soft.

Above all, when you go to the hills, step true,
For your legs are your life.
Look the dangers in the eye,
For they need sane evaluation.
Laugh at the hardships,
For they entertain or evict you.
And revel in the cold and discomfort,
For it builds your manly soul.

Now if these words find root in your soul
And your soul finds it's home in the hills,
You will be a bushman and a mountain man.
You will buffet life's storms,
And shape its weather over the miles.

©2014

At Home in the Hills – by James Jordan
Published by Fatherheart Media 2014
First Published 2002

PO Box 1039, Taupo, New Zealand 3330
www.fatherheart.net

Printed in the USA/NZ

ISBN: 978-0-9941016-3-1

All rights reserved. No part of this publication may be reproduced, stored in a retrieval system, or transmitted in any form or by any means – for example, electronic, photocopy, recording - without the prior written permission of the publisher. The only exception is brief quotation in printed reviews.

For other books, e-books, teaching, CD, DVD or MP3 of James Jordan please visit www.fatherheart.net/shop. Online international orders welcome. International shipping available.

Contents

Miro Valley	10
Introduction	16
1. A Boy's Dream	23
2. The Hunter Emerges	31
3. The Green Novice	43
4. Ross, a True Friend	55
5. Eels, Cowpies and Off-centre Things	69
6. Stray Bullets, Stray People	79
7. Lonely Times	97
8. The Odd Few Deer	111
9. Bad Weather	135
10. One Day in Fiordland	159
11. A Few More Odd Deer	175
12. The Hunter Becomes the Hunted	207
13. New Horizons Open Up	219
14. Changes in The Hills	233
Epilogue	248

Miro Valley

Miro Valley spreads out below me to the East as a shallow bush clogged and wide depression some two miles long and a mile wide. To the north of the valley the creek drops first over a waterfall some eighty feet high and then in a series of gorges and waterfalls which I haven't explored fully even yet. It continues to drop for a mile or more another thousand feet to the Pahiatua plains and the rich farmland that flanks these Tararua Ranges all along it's eastern side.

To the south of Miro valley another creek has its beginnings. It first meanders along through some high clearings about its edges until a mile or so downstream it drops over a huge waterfall. Being two hundred or more feet high surrounded by high cliffs on all sides the fall here is a formidable barrier to anyone coming upstream into the valley. From there it makes its way again through many gorges and twisting, falling cataracts, deep high sided pools and impassable barriers until it finds it's way out onto the Manawatu Plains.

A ridge covered with a blanket of dark green scrub six to ten feet high is the boundary of the eastern side of the valley. The major characteristic of this bush is its ability to matt together its brittle dense branches into a solid wall of almost impregnable wood and leather like, thick scratchy leaves. It is sometimes easier to swim on top of these vast areas of undulating amazing foliage than to press through or squirm under them. Leatherjacket is usually avoided by all when it is fully matured.

On this western side of Miro valley the ridge is somewhat easier being only very sparsely dotted with leatherjacket bushes yet except on the last slopes of what has always been known to me as Bull Knob, where it is as dense as anywhere in this country. But in most places pepper wood scrub has the dominance and through the old clearings that are slowly disappearing to its encroaching creep our old track is still useable. This is the only realistic entrance to Miro

Valley, yet even from here most curious wanderers would discard any notion of venturing down into it. Miro Valley is not beautiful. It's hundreds of Miro trees raise their rounded and dark green heads, shaped by years of strong winds, to all point solidly eastward, over a tangle of secondary growth bush which never attains any real height and grandeur. Beneath it is a jungle of undergrowth that reaches to the lower branches of the highest trees throughout its unique length.

To drop into this valley from where I am seated here at The Rocks; a place we named overlooking Miro Valley, requires clambering through hundreds of metres of scrub as you head downhill. You are scratched by clinging bushlawyer vines that rip at your clothes, legs and face and climb under, over and around old rotting stumps and tangles of logs whilst only being able to see short metres ahead all the time. That is, of course, unless you know the old simple track that my friends and I cut many years ago that has always been obscure and could have been crossed many times by rare visitors and never noticed. Even after hundreds of metres of travel into the valley from the ridge here your vision amongst the trees of Miro Valley will probably never be more than fifty metres or so at best: mostly only twenty.

The valley has two streams running out of it as I have said; one flows more or less to the north and the other to the south. One runs out on the eastern side of the Tararua Mountain Range and the other on the west. Therefore the centre of the valley where the final fingers of each of these two creeks ease towards each other but never touch, is in fact the main divide of the Tararuas. However here in Miro Valley that watershed is not a ridge, as it would be pictured. It is the wide and only imperceptibly raised bottom of this unusual valley. To cross that watershed from one creek to the other is an orienteers nightmare. In the dense and low bush of the watershed area the high ridges on each side of the valley can't be seen to give bearings. The intricate intertwining of the two streams myriad fingers are unable to be defined from one another and are often only metres apart but one can't be seen from any other. Each one, that looks almost exactly like all the others, may lead the opposite direction to where you want to go. I have never mastered the lie of this knot of waterways even though I have spent literally months living on its verge. Four hunters who wandered into this valley once intending to only spend four or five hours here, wandered about on this watershed becoming totally disoriented and finally decided after two days to simply head downstream to the plains on the farmland. They had no idea where downstream would lead them except that it must lead them out of the high country on one side of the range of the Tararuas or the other. It took them another two days to finally get out to the plains. It was a distance of five miles. It had taken them two hours to get to the point where they became disoriented and four days to get out.

Miro Valley is my place. I first dropped down into this valley in nineteen sixty-five when I was only fifteen. I had heard from older men that somewhere in its depths some hunters had built a hut down there and I was inspired to find it. After three day trips into it's interior I finally found that hut, which it's forgotten builders ceased to use, and over the next years learned many of Miro Valley's secrets. I don't know them all even yet. I found a unique deep amphitheatre under the leatherjacket belt just this year that I didn't previously know about.

I saw my first wild deer here and shot my first one too in a small clearing in the leatherjacket on the furthest ridge that we named the Back Ridge. The hut down below became my home in the hills. The many deer antlers there, covered with moss and rotting on and near the punga wall, were mostly killed with my rifle. On the track we cut from the hut to this ridge I sweated under many heavy loads of venison. Those two Moreporks that you now hear from the beds inside the hut as nightfall closes are the young of others that I have heard in the past who are in turn are the young of others that I have been lulled to sleep by in my youth. The old stag that I shot yesterday on the clearing in the Toko' stream, which empties out onto the Manawatu plains to the west, is probably the grandson of one that noted my silent passing years ago. His antler formation was typical of many that I have seen in Miro Valley over the years.

In the valley to the south, just below the big waterfall, a tributary from the back ridge drops into the main stream on the true left. It falls over many drops and through ancient logjams making travel through there extremely difficult if not impossible. It is impossible to enter from the main river. However there is access into that little and hidden valley from above and it is that stream in particular that I own as mine. I only know of one other person who has dipped their boots into that water and seen something of its lie. I went there with my son Matt last year. It's a simple, sweet and hidden place beyond the valley of little appeal. Even I haven't been there very often but I claim it as mine and accept ownership as only a hunter would, as I am the only claimant. It was there that I erected and left my fly camp during some of the weeks of my meat hunting times during the late nineteen sixties. Several deer fell to my Sako .243 rifle there and I carried them for many hours to sell to provide me with more money to live in my valley longer. I sweated with many loads of up to, and occasionally over, two hundred pounds on the steep side of the little valley. From there over the ridge to the main Toko' stream and then up the track we had cut to the point called Scrub and on down to the farmland where my car waited. Its cold desolate motor and cold gray paint always seemed to match the mood I felt arriving back to this article of civilization whose temperamental moods could cause despair and frustration. It was never my friend.

But Miro Valley was and is more than a friend. It has always been a home in the hills and a warm and familiar place. It was a refuge from people in general; who I never seemed to be at ease with except two close friends who came to Miro Valley guided by me at first. In fact they never came here without me.

Miro Valley was the place where I first faced the issues of manhood. Overcoming fear, aloneness and hard physical demands without help. I learned to navigate my own way, to make decisions that my well being depended on, as well as look after my own needs of food, warmth and shelter. To sleep satisfied in warmth and comfort after having killed, cleaned, carried, cooked and consumed your own meal is a satisfaction in manhood of deep consequence.

I not only explored much of the valleys secret beauties of glade, waterfalls and chasms but also my own inner realities of thought, ideal and belief. Many don't know what they consist of inside their own inner being and it takes solitude, silence and simplicity of living to see these deep resources surface. It is not what we think or do that makes up what we are; it is the things that float up from deep within. "Out of the heart are the issues of life", the writer of the Biblical book of Proverbs says. Many never take the time to look below the surface of the feelings and reactions they notice wafting out of their inner being. So they never know who they are. This valley not only shaped me but it helped me to know my shape.

I look at Miro Valley now from this hillside with the perspective of over thirty years of life since I first made those fearful steps off this very ridge into the thick tangle of its interior. I was fearful of not being able to make the ridge again and become lost for days not knowing north and south in a panic of despair. My boots have done those fearful steps again and again over the last thirty years but in such a variety of ways and in so many places. This valley was the first step of a lifestyle of ventures. It provided a prototypical situation that I have duplicated many times. If I had not done what

I did back when I was a boy of fifteen by leaving this ridge to search for the hidden hut in the fearful and unknown reaches below, not only would I have never found the hut, valley, and adventures I enjoyed there, but I would not have developed the courage to do what I do now in my life and work. I travel much of the world constantly now and new situations arise regularly. There have been many steps into 'new and dark valleys' along the way. But these feet of mine cannot be held back now and I don't see mountain peaks ahead. Only continuous slopes climbing away into the unknown beyond the horizon. It is the way of my life.

So a pattern was started here in this place so humbly called Miro Valley. I am gladder of it than I can say. I will always remain grateful to having had this valley as my home, and to me it will always be home. I came from here and it was here that I became a man. I have gone forth from these beginnings into the world. If I considered myself to be a knight going forth to do good with sword and steed I would have to name myself firstly as James, Knight of Miro Valley. Here I found my armour and steed. Here I killed my lion and bear. Here I looked myself in the mirror. Here I found a home in nature, and confidence about my place in it.

However there is another chapter to the story. It was another place and time, another reality and existence and another manhood and teacher that, added to all of this, moulded me to a greater fullness without which no person is complete. But that is another story. It doesn't in any way eclipse what Miro Valley has developed in me but this valley adds to what the other story establishes. To really know me you must know both. This book tells the full story of the foundation of my manhood in the hills and the beginning of the other story that must wait for another book to complete, if it is ever complete.

Introduction

Hobbling on the tender white and soft skin of my bare feet in this small area of crisp frost covered grass and wood chips outside the door of Waterfall Creek hut is taking a certain amount of self discipline. It is a chill, still and cloud free mid spring dawning in the midst of the mountains of New Zealand. I slowly raise the over full bowl of precious water I am carrying higher and higher until, holding it well above my head I tilt it slowly and its steaming warmth runs onto my head and cascades luxuriously down over my naked body. It washes the soap suds thickly scrubbed into my skin to my feet and replaces the tight and tingly goose bumpy sensation that was gripping me all over with exhilarating, glorious, relaxing and luxurious heat.

The high tussock ridges of the Hikurangi Range shine golden as creeping morning rays of sun begin to burn into them lighting them up to an unnatural sharpness, and towering out of lower slopes of deep green beech forest, the whole mountain valley smiles steeply down on me. The joy of life and the comradeship of the mountains spectacular presence fills me to the brim.

My exultant YEEEEE HOOO HOOO HOOOOOOOOO, boldly pierces the freezing silence down the valley. This is a reminiscing trip and I have two weeks to poke around the old haunts where twenty-eight years of nostalgia have built a magical aura in my mind. Over the years I have been back a few times for shorter periods of a few days but those brief times didn't give me the feelings of what it is like to live in the mountains as I once had, now some years ago.

The last few days saw me stopping briefly overnight at the recently renovated Kelly Knight hut where those years ago I spent time professionally hunting when there was only a tent camp there. Brilliant sunshine flooded the Pourangaki Valley as

I wandered up river wading through the deeper pools to the Pourangaki Hut where I settled in for a few days easy hunting and exploring in that massive and steep valley.

During those days an awkward fall in the gorge in the upper Pourangaki River cracked two of my ribs giving me a few very uncomfortable days and nights bound to the hut. With the help of a group of hunters that arrived in a helicopter I stayed on and was able to continue as long as I didn't twist my body in certain ways. My pack weight and its shoulder straps didn't affect those ribs and so on I went. Nothing is going to stop me from having this time back where my heart has drawn me and life has given me the opportunity to savour. The pain is lessening now and I am even able to yell aloud in joy at being here.

Crossing the high mountain divide between the Pourangaki and Kawhatau rivers I was blasted with high winds cannoning up from the South and whipping the tussock mercilessly. It is a wonder it was able to withstand the onslaught and not be ripped from the poor soils and shale where its roots had penetrated and then I am sure were holding on for dear life. After dropping off the main ridge into the calmness of the northern lee side of this part of the Hikurangi Range, known by hunters of yesteryear as the Eastcoast spur, the distant speck of Waterfall Creek Hut became visible way down in the valley below me on the forks where the creek does a small and unusual horseshoe bend. Early summer warmth striking the north facing slopes reflected off the trickling water, which fell over white rocks under a faultless blue sky, and I picked my way downwards over the crumbling country into the ever-widening valley. Briefly stopping beside some overhanging yellow seed heads of a clump of flowering Spanish Speargrass plants I stripped down to warm weather clothing placing the extra that had been needed on the tops, under the flap of my pack. The coldness of the Pourangaki slopes had been well replaced there and my pack and rifle and I enjoyed the change.

I woke this morning to a white moonlit landscape of frost and a clear sky promising a fine day again but also had the nagging feeling of stickiness of a body that had not been washed for several days. Early shades of gray peeking into the valley as night darkness receded discovered me zigzagging across the wide shingle flats picking up lengths of driftwood here and there in arms clad in a polarfleece bush shirt from which protruded two cold and fast moving bare legs. My shoulders were hunched to voice protest against the cold air that always seems to be able to find ways to slip its icy fingers down your neck or around your vulnerable belly.

After smashing the lengths of wood with an axe head welded onto a piece of pipe that serves its ungainly life at the hut, a match under a pillow sized crumple of dead beech leaves and twigs soon had the fire blazing. Its flames leapt right up the chimney filling the fireplace from side to side as only a fire built solely with white, light and bone dry driftwood can. Soon three of the huts biggest billies were frizzing around the edges where the superheated extremities of cold water butted to tortured billy rims. Then the rewarding deep gurgle and frothing of water boiling hard filled the hut and the moment to undress had arrived. Not without some apprehension on a cold morning like this I can tell you.

My second YEEEEEE HOOOOOOOOOO as the warm water hits me is a more calculated one and it seems the mountains respond with an understanding nod of peaceful yet excited agreement. Whistling a tune that I like but can't reproduce properly I pull on my clean hut clothes and then use the remainder of the hot water to scrub and rinse the others that have been on my back over the last days climbing on the hill. After hanging them out on a wire twitched to two frost encrusted manuka shrubs I wipe my bent comb free of pack dust from the recesses of a pocket and my hair soon assumes the orderly pattern I am used to. I feel wonderfully fresh and ready for a day of rest and reading with perhaps a short hunt in the afternoon.

Making a brew my teaspoon clanks against the inside of my tin mug as I stir a hot half pint of sweet tea and then amble over to and sit under a small perfectly formed beech tree standing slightly apart from the mass of others on the flat and up the surrounding hills. This position overlooks the river that walks this way and that over the receding flats. In this picture painting setting between steep and massive slopes my mind begins to wander and various questions and thoughts flow through. This is home for me. I feel more, me, here, than anywhere else I know. Not this spot in particular but this environment. I love the hills and being in them. How has this happened to me? Why am I different to others that I know who may enjoy nature but which is for them merely a nice place to visit and that's all? For me it is a place where I receive strength. Life seems to make sense to me more here than anywhere. Somehow civilization seems to be a blight on the face of life to me and this place seems to be the way life should be. This is real.

Yet a man can't live here continuously. We all need people unless we are damaged internally. We eventually become deranged if we live alone too long. I know. You can't survive off a place like this either. Food needs to be carried here with you from where you brought it in civilization. Life here needs civilization there. Yet this solitude and this wilderness are so invigorating. It seems to nurture me and feed me with the will and the ability to go on and survive the rat race that I have to return to be a part of. Being here and knowing that here is still here when I'm not here makes me able to even thrive in the centre of civilization. What I feel about life in the hills is something of a quandary even to me. I don't know exactly how it all fits into that other life that is also important to me but seems to be diametrically opposed. But then why try to understand it all if it's all working together well. All I know is that I love the hills and being here is more than something that I enjoy. It's a part of my inner being.

   Sitting here in the growing warmth of the day with the view reaching some miles down the valley towards the Mokai Patea Range and McKinnon Hut where I made my first venture into these Ruahine Ranges over thirty years ago I think back over the years. I am glad that I have retained what fitness I have so that I can wander these places with pack and rifle still. I know it is always possible to fly into these isolated places now by helicopter but that is not how I am used to experiencing the hills. I like packing in and make the miles as I always have, and will do so as long as I can.

   I'm thinking over some of the good times that the hills had given me, of some of the people that I have known and things that have happened. Occurrences that are simply a hunters stories to those that I have related them to over the years but to me are now the valuable steps that I have climbed, some of the building blocks of my life. The first book that I read of New Zealand hunting as a young and good keen man was Newton McConochie's; "You'll learn no harm from the Hills". It's a good and true statement all by itself without even having a book following it. I have only learned good from my times in the hills.

   In this book I have tried to communicate what the hills have been to me and are to me with you that may read this and find similar things in yourself. The fellowship of hunters and men and woman of the hill. It contains my journey into friendship with Jesus Christ and the love of His Father and ours. That friendship and love has taken me all around the world and to thousands of people imparting to them the knowledge of God that gives our lives a center from which we find a fulfillment that completes every part of us.

This is a book mainly of stories of experiences that I have had with some poems thrown in. I have found that these two ways of words communicate not only the facts of an incident but, especially poems, communicate something of the experience of the heart. Facts and stories are cold and empty things until the addition of the experience of the human heart gives them atmosphere and feeling. It is from the heart, the writer of the book of wisdom states in Proverbs, flow the issues of life. Life is more than interests, incidents and accomplishments. Life is how the heart of a person is affected and developed through those incidents and endeavors. Happenings pass into memories but the effect of them changes you for the rest of your life. The growth of the person.

I hope that this book will cause something in you to grow too.

Chapter One
A Boy's Dream

❦

I was an eight-year-old boy when I first saw the Hikurangi Ranges. They loomed up to an impossible height above and ahead of us, brilliantly white against the darkened clouds of a sky that frowned down at the land that it had tormented over the last few days. We had heard that there had been a heavy fall of snow on the foothills of the Ruahines and my parents were taking us kids out to see the snow for the first time.

As we rounded a bend in the narrow one way metal road, this magical view struck us all, I'm sure, but it pierced so deeply in me that it became a base for the rest of my life. Framed in the windscreen of our little navy blue Ford Anglia, I and my family rattled and swayed our way out the devilishly windy and narrow Kawhatau Valley road in the winter of 1958. Peering between the shoulders of my mother and father and being jostled by my older brother and sister in the cramped back seat of the car, which probably kept us warm, I couldn't take my eyes off the snow covered tops of the Mangaweka and Hikurangi peaks, that loomed up and towered over us in the near distance.

As the youngest and smallest, I was closed off in a cocoon of my own thoughts and dreams, caught in the magic and wonder of my first sight of snow and the unbelievable images that high mountain peaks look to a small boy. It is my first memory of mountains, and was my first experience of the drawing power of the wilderness that has continued to be with me over the near forty years since. Little did I know what that particular magical Range would mean to me in the years following. We never made it to the snow that time as, rounding a bend a little further on, we were faced with a mudslide that had come down over the road just before our arrival. This turned us reluctantly back to Mangaweka and home and probably a maire fire to warm us all up again.

It was in the barber's chair a year or so later when I first heard the term 'deer culler'. The barber at Mangaweka, a man named Ken Dowling, who knew the Ruahine Ranges like the proverbial back of his hand, was giving me my short back and sides. Ken had hunted widely in the Ruahines with a blanket and rifle, sleeping under the stars in the then much more isolated and untravelled hills that have now come into the helicopter age of instant wilderness. The hills have changed a lot since the days of choppers. The feeling you have in them that is. The atmosphere that you sense in them is different, it's not the hills themselves that have changed.

I sat, a small skinny boy in the big shiny leather and varnished wooden chair, while Ken was talking to Len Bosher, a local farmer, about a recent deerstalking trip he had been on. Len asked him how the trip had gone and Ken said that there had been few deer in the area because the government deer cullers had been through and cleaned the area out. I learnt three things in that intense moment and a dream formulated that commanded the next ten years of my life, and influences me still. One, that men live in those magic mountains that I had seen a year or so earlier. Two, that they live there to shoot deer, and three that they are great hunters. I thought the words 'Deer Culler' were

A Boys Dream

spelt 'Deer Colour' and that only added to the fantastic picture that was being built up in my mind. From that time on the only thing that I wanted to be was a "Deer Colour".

My mother was, at that time well known amongst the farmers of Mangaweka for her love of and ability at rabbit shooting. I still own the B.S.A. single shot twenty-two that she bought second hand for nine pounds and with which she shot thousands of rabbits. It was normal for her to get fifty or sixty in an afternoon and I know that many of the rabbits that she shot were headshot for she figured that if you aimed for the head then you either missed cleanly or you had a clean kill. My Mum considered that Bob Kidd, the local rabbiter, a profession that I later spent a few years at, was a better shot than her but in the town she was known as a crack shot. My father had won the school shooting trophy at New Plymouth Boys High when he was there. Among the people that I lived with shooting was a part of life and if you were a person worth your salt you had to be able to shoot. To me, deer colours must be the best and I wanted to be one and live in those mountains.

We left Mangaweka when I was eleven and went to live just out of Palmerston North at Linton. It seemed that life had taken a cruel turn for me. There were no hills or bush in sight of the place where we lived, only the tamed and suffocated land of farms, crops, cows and sheep. I feel that land needs to be free to be itself and still enjoy fenceless and uncultivated land best.

School had lost much of its interest and my inner life closed in on me. I was alone and lonely but for two close friends who were twins. The next years passed slowly till one day my brother, a ham radio enthusiast a few years older than me, was invited by the local Search and Rescue Dept. of the Police Force to go on a practice search. He came back with stories of the mountains, bush tracks, tussock, packs, rain, cloud covered peaks, boots and the ridges and rivers of the nearby Tararua Ranges. I'm sure that my family didn't realize how fascinated I was with those stories that he told. I came alive again inside but not for the things that my dad wanted me to be concerned for. He wanted me to do well at school, which I certainly had the ability to do, earn good qualifications, save for a future house and section, and move up the ladder of success in the market place. I wanted to be a 'Deer Colour'.

MAGICAL MCKINNON

I heard through a friend of a friend that a group were starting a new tramping club, and so happened to go along to the first meeting of the Palmerston North Tramping and Mountaineering Club. From there I had my first experience in the hills proper. We climbed up the gutbusting bush face from the Crion Station onto the Hikurangis, where I had seen the snow some seven years before as a boy, and in heavy snow and bright sunshine clambered our way to McKinnon Hut on the northern end of the range. The crust on the top of the snow lost its firmness as the day progressed and we kept falling through it up to our thighs. It was an exhausting day. At one point, on the last steep decline down to the hut, I fell through the three feet of snow, my feet hit the pressed down tussock and slid downhill and I disappeared right under the soggy stuff. The others, in exhausted hysteria, had to help dig me out.

It was a full moon that night and although it was cold I stood at the door of the hut as long as I could. I absorbed the full impact of moonlight, silent on bulges of snow covering the tussock slopes, snow laden stunted beech trees of the upper bus hedge, and the mysterious beckoning of the Mokai Patea Range silhouetted to the north across the Kawhatau river which could barely be heard murmuring in the stillness of the night so far below. This is a memory that is as clear now as it was a vision then. Finally my tiredness and the cold drove me to resign myself to the

A Boys Dream

crampedness of the hut's interior, its noisy, bustling, tramping-hyped inhabitants, and the privacy of my inadequate sleeping bag. I couldn't afford a good sleeping bag so I learned to sleep cold in those days, and it has been a great advantage ever since.

`Seven of us in the six bunk hut meant that the two youngest of us had to sleep top and tail in the one bed, and it was a long night for my friend and I. Suddenly, in the shadows of the hut, accentuated by shafting moonlight streaming in the regulation two windows, Trevor, ever the keen man, was up. With a clattering of billies, snapping of twigs and a crackling of flames the billies were slung for breakfast. Midst the dark interior corners of the hut, muffled voices reluntantly tried to sound like good keen men from the intimacy of Twenty Belows and Everest sleeping bags. I couldn't believe that it was morning already. It seemed that I had just gone to bed, but Trevor insisted that it was five o'clock and time to be up and at it. With pretended eagerness and blatant noneagerness, five bleary-eyed staggering mother's boys dragged themselves out of their scratchers and began to try to look alive and fit.

Unconvincingly they attempted to get into the act of being good keen trampers hoeing into billies, fire, water, swannies, bush shirts, etc. I was still enjoying the warmth of my cocoon, trying to delay opening my eyes. The porridge was cooked and being dished up when someone asked what the time was. Fifteen minutes later we were all back in our bags and mostly asleep. Trevor had mistaken the hands on his watch and what he thought was five o'clock was in fact twenty five past twelve. He was not popular for a while that night but, as always happens the hardships and mistakes of life in the hills, although evicting the phony mountain men, entertain the true.

On the way through the almost white-out conditions the next day, I saw, for the first and only time so far, a completely circular

At Home in the Hills

rainbow with my own shadow in its centre. I read a name for that once and determined to remember it, but didn't. We plodded up the slope from McKinnon hut to the top of the ridge, stepping in the night hardened footprints of compacted snow, and made our long way down to Crion Station and the vehicles. Our footprints were the only thing that we could see most of the way along the ridge as the world looked like the inside of a huge white table tennis ball. No depth of field, no distance perception and very little up or down. It was cold and we were all tied up in as many clothes as we could muster. I don't think that the build up of adrenaline in my system from the excitement of that weekend finally left me for some weeks.

McKinnon was a place so wonderful, remote and mysterious to me then but is now a dear familiar friend whose secrets I know well. Many deer have fallen to my rifle in the nooks and crannies of those hillsides.

My mind is full of such memories, as it is for all whom have a part of their souls permanently living in the mountains and the mountains implanted in them. The hills, as the mountains of New Zealand are affectionately know, are a place where dreams are born, lived and never forsaken. We are either of those who escape into the hills from the stresses of life or we are of those who venture into the world from our home in the hills. One of the cullers that I later shared some huts with said that I was a dreamer and I guess that's true if it means I see wonder in all the details of our wilderness and become rapt in the vistas and experiences the hills have alone to give. That wonder, and the rapture thereby produced, has created for me a home in the hills.

It's funny to watch people new to the hills cringe at the first boot full of ice water as they cross a river of melted snow early in the morning. Or to see them try to skirt around dew drenched fern or tussocks to keep their shorts dry as we move off before

A Boys Dream

dawn to a long day on the hill. You grow to accept these things as a part of well compensated for, whole. Then they become familiar experiences that warm your soul, and finally they become the warm friends that tell you that you are home.

I remember a guy that came on a trip on Labour weekend in 1966 who couldn't take the entertainments of the hills. I guess I might have seen it differently if the joke had been played on me. As we were leaving the cars at the road end, near the Makaroro River, someone put three stones about the size of softballs in his pack without his knowledge. He carried those stones up the Makaroro River, up the three to four thousand foot climb of Colenso track, over Te Atuamahuru and down the wonderful ride of a long shingle slide into the Mangatera River where we stopped for the night at Remutupo Hut.

This hut was later taken to Ruahine Corner by helicopter to replace the second one that was erected on that site. I never saw the original hut at Ruahine Corner but would love to see a photo of it someday. When he found the stones as he was taking his gear from his pack at Remutupo he was not amused, to say the least. He wasn't good company the next day either. It snowed on the morning of the day that we walked out over the tops again. We zigzagged our way back up the huge shingle slide just above Remutupo hut in the light snow onto the main range. A beautiful time walking through this wonderland.

A deer culler I worked with later, name of Chris Satherly, saw our tracks from the distance on the big slip and remembered them well enough to mention them to me a few years later. However, when we arrived back at the cars there was another outburst from our companion. As he unpacked his pack, he found the same stones in there again. I never found out who did it and I don't know if he did either, but we never saw him again on another tramp. The hardships and tricks of the hills and its travelers are the entertainments of the wilderness. If you can enjoy them you will be at home there.

I only did a few trips with the fledgling P.N.T.M.C. My two friends and I learnt enough to be able to read maps and tie our boots up, so we devised trips faster and more interesting than the club could. We were soon logging up an impressive list of huts, ridges and rivers that we were familiar with. We belonged to the rip, snort and bust brigade then, and we tried to set new speed records every time we went along tracks that we had been on before. An hour and fifteen from Ohau to South Ohau, skinning an unlucky young goat on the way. Thirty-five minutes running all the way to the Punga Hut, a trip that usually took an hour and fifteen.

One time, racing down off Girdlestone Saddle to South Ohau hut enroute from the hut at Avalanche Flats, we spotted a large group of trampers ahead milling around in bewilderment. When four of them sighted us they ran up the track to us shouting out, "Do you know where we are?" They had come down from Te Matawai hut through the bush expecting to hit Girdlestone Saddle, but had missed the ridgetop and had been bush bashing for some time, finally resting, although they hadn't realized that they were in fact in the centre of the track. They were lost, right on the track, and the ones that had run up to us were panicking. Trying to hide our bewilderment at their ridiculous predicament, we nonchalantly pointed out the brilliant white and red track markers clearly seen on the trees all around. Their wide-eyed relief and calls of thanks, that seemed to come from souls reprieved from hell, followed us as we, with casual heroism, continued speedily on our way.

I was gaining experience, slowly but still had a long way to go.

Chapter Two
The Hunter Emerges

❧

In the early weeks of my tramping experiences, with the Palmerston North Tramping and Mountaineering Club, two events occurred that defined me for the years ahead. One addicted me to the wonderful wild red deer, and the other to the homes that we make and find in the isolation of the hills. The love of these two is the foundation of the hunter.

Gold Creek

It was a dim winter day with cloud only a few hundred feet above our heads as we walked over aged, sour and weathered grasses of the western Hawkes Bay. There had been a heavy fall of snow extending well down onto the farms in the last few days, and, although it had only dampened and compressed every plant on the flats, the bush was clogged with it. Four of us were trying to find a track the map insisted headed off the farmland at the top of a clear ridge, over into Gold Creek on the eastern side of the main Ruahine Range. We were not able to find it and so we just headed up a little beautifully forested creek hopefully to find an easy way over the ridge, and drop into the Gold Creek hut. The boulders and fallen logs in the creek bed were gently covered with rounded snow hummocks, and the bright clear water of the stream, trickling between the stones, could be seen from time to time in the dark recesses of intricate ice formations along the water's course. The trees on the stream's steep sides, occasionally extending overhead, covered with winter's paint, were a continuously revealed series of more and more beautiful Christmas cards. It was an absolute fairyland.

In the little creek the snow became deeper and deeper. Sometimes our thighs were pushing the snow away and we were all four feeling the effects of the effort. Finally, leaving what had become impossible travel in the creek and heading up the ridge, we began to come across fresh deer tracks - I remember a spot where a deer had obviously lain down for the night. A shallow hollow in the snow, exposing at its centre the fallen leaves of the previous autumn, gave the distinct message of a shivering animal getting as much warmth as possible from tightly tucked up limbs, huddled in this beautiful yet forbidding place.

Then all of a sudden Trevor, I don't remember his last name now, said from in front of me "Look." There in the snow clogged bush only about twenty yards away, on a gently sloping ridge, was a young red deer spiker. It was the first deer that I had ever seen, and all my other senses ceased, pouring their energies into my eyes, so that they took an internal soulograph, clear, sharp and deeply etched to the full extent of my soul's photographic capacity.

There were no deer farms in those days and I had never seen a deer apart from photos. This wonderful animal was looking at us. I could see his deep brown eyes examining us with interest, although caution smouldered in the surrounding lines of his innocent face above the damp patch of his nose-tip and nostrils. His ears were flicking and focusing on us, trying to assess us. His smooth and even coat, auburn on his back and ribs, flowed into dark browns at the neck and tops of the legs, and lower down jet black against the snow which his hooves had pierced and that spread all around. He was looking alert and toey, and his nose was searching the air trying to catch our scent. It was magnificent. It was a wild stag, young and free. I loved that young stag. It seemed to embody all that the mountains in their mystery and massiveness, the rivers in their coldness, beauty and power, and the bush in its hidden secrets and dangers, held and had lured me to experience. It stood there for an age that lasted two seconds but still exists. That moment sealed a destiny in me. From then till now, part of me lives in the wilds of the New Zealand bush and mountains. It is my home too, as it was for that young stag, and is for many other New Zealanders that have had that deep touch of the wild on their souls. I wrote a poem about that day but the real poetry is in my soul.

Gold Creek Spiker

Knee deep snow, fresh, purest white.
Laden beech trees bowed.
Silent trampers stroll the heights,
Warm coats and boots, woolen hats.
Up the mountain in thick cloud,
Way beyond the flats.

White so white and silent, still
New beauty every yard.
Filled with awe yet more to fill,
But move on, on and up,
Plow through soft snow breathing hard,
Great draughts from natures cup.

*Leave the creek now up the spur,
In thigh deep drifts we see,
A Morepork dazzled by our blur,
He perches blinking hard.
Cameras click, he changes tree
His new post now to guard.*

*Then round a spur and look, a deer,
In snow choked beech forest frame.
Perfect coat, clear eyes and ear,
He watches then he turns.
Oh stay! But no, a crushing shame
My heart within me burns.*

*A merest glimpse, my dream had come,
This spiker fleeting find.
Of worldly joys he was the sum,
A wild stag young and free.
I live with him now in my mind
Where only I can see.*

It is an amazing paradox to some that the one who can experience such feelings over a meeting with an animal like that can also be a hunter of the same animal. One of the quandaries of life. I don't profess to be able to explain it any more than a man can explain why he loves the sea that kills him. But my goodness that day was a memorable one for me.

Later I learnt that it is not a good idea to boil a billy on a primus situated under a snow-laden tree. The billy had almost boiled after much patience and shivering, this time on our part, all enduring in suffering silence, anxious for the reward of a hot brew. The sweat against our skin under our Swannys had almost turned to ice when the rising heat of the primus and our bodies dislodged the snow above. A great lump of it fell into the billy that we were tightly gathered around to deflect the wind from the flickering primus, but not as much as that which poured down our necks. Amidst the growls and sudden scrambling of four bodies all going in, not orderly directions, trying to escape the downpour of powdery all-invading whiteness dumping on us, the billy was violently overturned. That was one brew we never drank. It is also one experience that I have not repeated.

FINDING THE PUNGA HUT

For some time I had heard, from older bush men that I listened to, who talked of the mountains in a way that fascinated me, of a hut that was reputed to exist over the hills beyond the farthest farm boundary, backing onto a largely unknown part of the Tararua Ranges. Finding it appeared to be a mission of massive proportions to my fifteen-year-old ears. Only one of these men had ventured out to find this lost hut and had failed. Probably it was because they had insufficient time to look for it with their busy country lives. It sounded scary but I was keen to have a go and find the hut, perhaps becoming a man in the process.

The nearest farmer said that he knew the men that had built the hut and who went there regularly but that he didn't know exactly where it was. All I knew was that it was over that last bush clad ridge that was so often covered in cloud, and that seemed to tower over the farm in faint definition when the sky was blue but hazy in summer heat.

I borrowed our family's deep blue Morris Eight after convincing my Mum that I should, for safety's sake, carry her single shot BSA twenty-two. My Mum had been something of an Annie Oakley with that particular rifle, when rabbits had been plentiful in the nineteen fifties as I said earlier. Winding my way up the twisty Scotts road to the farmed plateau, I was soon following the sheep tracks in knee length grass tops to the bush edge off to the mysterious ridge dominating the skyline ahead. The farm was still being broken in and my friends Dennys and Robin Smith spent many of their weekends up there burning stumps and helping out, mending fences and the like. Those days are full of stories that would take a shelf full of books to do justice. The Army from Linton used to use the farm for what we called war games, and the antics that they got up to caused us endless entertainment.

From the bush edge there was a slow climb up through the old milled-over bush to the top of the ridge, on a track that had seen little use for many years. Twisting through clearings filled with clinging and tearing bushlawyer, over and round fallen logs already disappearing under the relentless spread of prolific summer growth, my happy face disregarded the scratches and trickles of blood appearing on my legs. At the top of the ridge I broke into a large clearing. Carefully noting a particular individual dead treetop at the beginning of the track for when I returned, I continued on the old track which took me through a small saddle and onto the skyline ridge. Miro Valley was then laid out before me, due east. Wide and shallow, my side of the valley dropped away through an endless expanse of jumbled trees, fading to a faint line where the centre creek must be. The far side of the valley, over a mile away, climbed up through tangled bush, mostly void of really tall trees, to little clearings where leatherjacket took over which crowned the peaks on the far side. For a youngster like me, the valley to the east was a fearful place to venture into alone.

The bush near the top of the ridge was a tangle of leatherjacket, pepperwood and dozens of other varieties of a similar ilk. It meant you could only see for two or three metres at a time, initially, near the ridge top. The undergrowth, predominantly of crown fern, often left no visual gap before the foliage of the trees took over, blocking the sky ten to fifteen metres above. Then, after three or four hundred metres it opened up into stuff that enabled you to see for ten to twelve yards though sometimes you could see for twenty. That is typical of the bush in that place and it was here that I learned my basic bush craft. A long fruitless day was ahead of me, poking and stumbling my way about the valley. It was late in the afternoon when my head popped out onto the ridge again and my eyes found the relief of long distance focus. Mount Egmont, as it was then called, appearing far out to sea over the curved sweep of the coast near Wanganui, could be seen as the sun began to dip towards it. It seemed to be a successful day. I had explored a maze-like jungle and returned to my starting point. It was a milestone in the development of my confidence in the bush. Fears faced dissipate in their own bluff. It was two years later that four guys were lost in that same valley for four days, walking out a few miles away while the search parties were still stamping around in the mist on those same slopes.

  Twice I headed into Miro Valley looking for the hut. I spent each day bush bashing around traveling from one creek to another with never a sign of humans. I did see my second deer though. I was following a small gutty creek down to the main stream in the centre of the valley, picking my way in the silence of the intricately beautiful waterway when I came to a small waterfall. It was really more like a water slide where a large rock, mostly covered by mosses, which spanned the side banks of the stream, allowed about a bucket of water every three or four seconds to slip down it's face, and suck and spray into a pool ten feet below. A couple of steps and a leap and I landed on the shingle flat gathered beside the bottom pool, the result of heavy rain and the last flood.

  The beauty of the spot is eternally hidden from all eyes but the hunter's by the complete covering of trees that spread over it. Its inaccessibility and the fact that it is situated on the way to nowhere – seem to guarantee its past and continuing solitary existence there in never ending privacy. As with many other places, I may be the only human to have ever passed through that particular spot.

Suddenly a loud "woof" exploded in the small shadowy glade at the base of the waterfall. I went cold with a rush of adrenaline that kept me shaking for the next half-hour or so. The hind that I hadn't seen amongst the pungas and that hadn't seen or heard me above the sound of the waterfall, crashed off into the punga draped shadows. I was left shaking all over with fright, adrenaline and excitement. Woo! The mountains, the bush, the wild deer, the creeks, the aloneness, the adventure, even the scratched legs and tiredness all added up in that moment to an immense high of exhilaration. Woo! And it's all mine. Sitting down I went over every inch of that moment and the picture of that hind is, even now, still on my memory. Occasionally I can still smell that moment. The atmosphere and impact it made on me as a fifteen-year-old, can still drift back out of the years, from the recesses of my subconscious, and thrill me again and again. That's the joy of the hunter. The memory! I have no idea if the telling of these stories can possibly convey what they have meant and mean to me.

However, it was the third trip that turned up the sought for reward. Another day of bush bashing and I was tired and scratched and exhausted. I was learning what it was to spend many hours alone without talking, and yet experience many wonders.

The time wood pigeons merely sat on the branch while I approached to within feet of them. The time a silence in a more open spot under the trees felt alive, as if a deer had been there just seconds before I broke into it. What caused that feeling of not being alone when all of my senses said I was? A living silence. The time when the sun seemed to have suddenly leapt across the sky to the south of me instead of being in its normal place to the north. It was my internal compass that had become inverted, in fact, and what I felt was north was truly south. Getting that sorted out placed the sun in its true midday place to the north again.

The hunter's experiences are seen in his eyes. You can't see what he has seen in them but you can see that he has seen unique things. It's because he hasn't had another to see the things as he has seen them, and he has mulled them over and over in his mind and relished them alone. He knows that no one will ever be able to see what he has seen, feel what he has felt, or touch what he has touched, and so the things that have been prizes to his soul become stored inside him and no one can really appreciate them. Yet, you can see a reflection of his prizes in his eyes, if you have eyes to see it. Eyes that have seen gold look a little yellow to the one who values gold. Eyes that have seen some of the wonders of the hills have the touch of the wide open spaces in them. Hunters recognize it in each other's eyes, and they can weigh each other up in an instant.

When outdoor people meet they glance with nonchalant intensity at each other's eyes where the true message of who they are is revealed, all the while going about the formalities of common, although usually sparse, conversation and the physical rituals of stance and expression. These all indicate their values, experience and kind.

There are many kinds of hunters. Weekend hunters. Bush edge hunters. Spotlighters. Egotistical cowboys. Genuine youngsters. Rich shooters with magnums, etc., etc., etc., without end. And then there are guys that simply love being there. Some are goons, some are simply after making a buck from the bush, some are sportsmen, and some true bushmen. The latter will help you all they can. To them the bush is almost holy. It's home. They know, love, and respect its ways, and can read the eyes of all the others.

Anyway, all that aside, there I was. My third trip into that valley

At Home in the Hills

had been much the same as the first two. Lots of bush bashing through miles of bush clad ridges and creeks, never seeing more than a few yards at a time. Finally I rested sitting on a stumpy, sun dried and bleached log, washed down by a long gone flood in the only true clearing, small at it was, that I'd come across in all my travels in that valley. I was eating mutton and tomato sauce sandwiches that I had made at the kitchen bench at home an hour or more before dawn that morning. Sandwiches that had been remodeled, in the now filthy sugar bag on my back, by the branches and logs they had brushed against during my travels. They still tasted good. Thinking of the long struggle up to the ridge again where I would start my trip home, I casually noticed that there was what looked like the start of a track on the other side of the little pool that my boots were in, while I soothed my feet.

Sandwich in hand, I squelched through the only unbroken stream of sunlight, and, sure enough it looked like a human track. On the tree there was a blaze! A few more yards along and, suddenly, out into the sunlight of a clearing of broad brown leafed grass and knee high pungas I stepped. There, just above me on a terrace backed by tall trees and a magnificent Rimu tree, the Punga Hut burst into sight. It looked just like a log cabin but made with pungas. There was a small nine-point stag's head on the gable end. A door made of poles and clear plastic ripped at the bottom challenged me from the far end. I approached cautiously. Maybe a wild pig had made the hut it's home and I would meet it rushing out as I went in.

It was eerie finding this hut in a valley that I had spent so much time in without seeing any sign of human presence. I felt strange around it at first. Later I spent many months here over the years, with friends and meat hunting alone. It became a home for me and a place where my friends and I grew up. There were no pigs in it. The interior smelt mouldy and the dirt floor dipped in the centre from the tramp of boots in the past. It seemed that the presence of people still lingered. The presence of strangers.

I finished my lunch leaning against the wall in the sunshine. I felt that I was a little taller. From the hut I could see a high point covered in leatherjacket to the north. It was the only reference point that I could latch on to for positioning the hut in the valley. In no other direction could I see anything significant to guide me back here. I knew of no tracks to or from the hut at that time. Later we discovered old tracks, and cut new ones, and the valley became well known to us. The different foliage and lay of the land became reference points in abundance. But, at that time, Bull knob, as we heard it called, became the only guide to the hut. Spotting it from different places in the valley, and comparing its aspect to the remembered aspect seen from the hut, I could travel the wide base of the valley, with its many small and contradictory streams, with confidence and ease. At least while it was daylight. I wrote this next poem about that day when I found the Punga Hut. One of the guys that built it was Rex Thompson. I ran into him some years later in Palmerston North and then knew his son Philip when I worked for the Manawatu Pest Destruction Board.

They say it's there beyond the last farm edge
Beyond the fences and the farthest ridge.
Beyond the hills and valleys tossed,
They say a hut hides lost,
And I went to seek its lonely ledge.

Two trips to the mountains beyond the farthest farm
I ranged alone in youthful fear of harm.
Through tangled bush and scratchy fern,

At Home in the Hills

Waterfalls all left astern
In vain to learn,
Of the hut that haunted the ranges calm.

Then on that trip, hours of wandering done.
Bruised and hungry, tired leg and lung.
Slumped in a clearing by some creek
Chewing sandwiches of meat
Thinking I'd need another week
I found it, and I and the mountains sung.

A faint trail led out of the creek by me,
And I plodded along a chain to see
The Punga hut burst into sight
In brilliant golden light
To the left and right.
A magic home in the mountains free.

The Punga Hut (1967).

Chapter Three
The Green Novice

❧

First Rifle

As soon as I turned sixteen I bought a Parker Hale Supreme three-o-three from Tisdalls in Palmerston North. It cost me twenty three hard earned pounds and fifteen hard to come by shillings and it was the prize of a lot of sacrifice and paying off on the hire purchase scheme. During lunch times I used to walk down from the high school that I went to, just to see it and handle its exotic lines. It seemed to be all that a rifle should be. It had the one thing that I still look for in a rifle - it fitted. When thrown to the shoulder the sights automatically lined up with my eye. Rifles with that characteristic have given me many deer over the years. I'm not a great shot. Probably about average, I would think. Though I've had my share of brilliance at times, often followed by periods that I couldn't hit anything. But, having a rifle that "fits" gives a person the best possibility of doing, at least, his best.

The day that I picked up that first three nought three was a great day. I carried it from the shop in a cardboard box to the car where my father sat waiting. Sitting next to him on the drive home, I ached to have this newly acquired, long awaited, item on my lap where I could run my hands along its smooth steel and polished wood. However, it simply lay in its box behind us on the back seat. I didn't want to act so emotionally in front of my dad. I now owned something that no one in my family had ever had. I was all set to be a deer hunter.

First Deer

The first four deer I killed fell on the same day, and I got three rounds of army three nought three ammunition for the stinky, maggot ridden ears that I handed over in a dirty sack to the forestry guys in a shiny office in town.

I had walked from our home at Linton, because my parents were away with the car. I left very early, in the dark, before the sun had edged the first touch of light over the tops of Te Mata trig on the north end of the foothills of our part of the Tararua Ranges. The most direct route to Scotts Road was across several farms, and I made my way through the farm tracks, along the creeks, and, artfully around the patches of bush, hoping I would not be sighted by any of the farmers as I was carrying a high powered rifle. I am sure it would have seemed inappropriate. However, I knew all of the farmers well, and that they would not have had a problem with me crossing their places.

Winding my way up the steady gradient of Scotts Road, I crested the top just on daybreak and was soon swinging my way to the north over the plateau country with my light gray pack bouncing happily on my back and my new rifle nursed comfortably in my hands. Finally the bush edge was in sight as I ploughed on out over the last farm. With that ten mile walk behind me, it had passed quickly, my thoughts were on getting to the hunting ground of Miro Valley and not on the effort of the walking I was doing. I rested briefly before starting the last leg of my journey to the Punga Hut that I had found a year or so before. Over the bush clad ridges and down into Miro Valley, I finally arrived at the secluded site beside the tiny creek. At the hut, surrounded by pungas and overseen by one solemn, mature Rimu tree with several smaller, silent sentries, that still stand there, the bush watches the occasional comings and goings of humans there. The miles had disappeared quickly to legs that were used to walking all day.

In the afternoon I hunted the ridge behind the hut, poking my nose about the clearings that occur occasionally between the bush and leatherjacket blankets that lay over the valley and butt up to each other, without encroaching. Three deer fell to four shots, and the sugar bag pikau on my back was loaded with the first meat that I had ever cut off a warm animal. Near one of the hinds that I shot, I slipped, and putting my hand to the ground to steady myself, I was surprised to see, next to my hand, the white spots and deep reddish brown of a fawn curled up in the broad leafed grasses bristling out of the ground on the clearing. I skinned it very poorly. It is still the only one I have ever found tucked away in its mother's hiding spot.

Making my way northward along the ridge during the afternoon and not knowing the valley well at that stage, I dropped down off the ridge into the creek too soon, and ended up caught between some waterfalls and an amazing gorge in the lower part of the stream. The afternoon was cooling into evening, I was in a place that I didn't know, and I began to get anxious about whether I could make it back to the hut before the darkness closed in, trapping me where I was. It was somewhere to the south of me, past this impossible tumble of huge rocks and cliff faces between which cold clear water leapt from height into bottomless dark holes lurking in the friendless shade of the gorge.

There's a kind of clammy fear that can overtake you when you're in the bush. You may find that you are not sure where you are, or find that you're not going to make it to shelter before dark. Until you have spent a night out in atrocious conditions and survived after all, this fear can be quite debilitating. From then on it's not such a fearful thing to get stuck out. It just takes a bit of effort to think coolly and evaluate the best place to camp. There is always a best place to camp or a best decision to make and, having done your best, you always feel better.

Finally, after continuous climbing and sidling ridges through thick and scratchy undergrowth, I dragged myself into the hut just on dark, with my trophies of ears and meat. There, I triumphantly settled down to spend my first night in the Punga Hut, more geographically alone than I'd ever been before. The feelings that pervaded my aloneness while eating my tea that night are indescribable. I had become a hunter - the fulfillment of a long-time dream, and the beginning of a life that I had claimed as mine.

I had discovered my own hunting ground without help: decided upon and bought my own rifle from my own earnings; had found, shot and butchered my deer alone in my own untrained way; had lit my own fire, and cooked and eaten my tea. I was happy with myself to say the least. Yet, night was closed in and I had never spent a night alone in the bush.

That first night there I overcame all fear of the dark that is naturally a part of us when we are young. I remember consciously enumerating all the things that could possibly happen to me in the dark, and from the bush, and, surprisingly, came up with a very short list. Crippling fear is so often based on the imagined rather than the real. When our emotions are locked to our logic, rather than our imaginations, I have found they are much more steady. I lay there on the bunk, consisting of poles with sacks slung between, feeling the isolation and the bush, outside in the dark, stretching the miles over the hills towards the farmland and home. A couple of Moreporks began to call to each other not far away, and, as they were a common sound to me in my childhood in Mangaweka, their familiar and friendly presence lulled me off to sleep. Those two Moreporks have followed me all around the backcountry, it seems, and great friends they have been to me too.

No one initiated me to the hills and hunting. I've learned almost all that I've come to know by experience alone in the bush, or with my friends that were as inexperienced as I was. Particularly my early adventures in the hills seemed more dangerous and massive in their challenge to me, because I knew of no one who had done this before. I was sixteen and felt these things with all the awe and imagination of a boy not yet fully a man. As I carried my pack and rifle the miles through the bush and across the hills of the farms back to Linton the next day, in the sunshine, I'm sure that I took slightly longer more confident paces, and saw the world from a higher elevation, as I reveled in the fact that I was now a deer hunter. I had taken a step to manhood. I was walking taller. My dream had become real.

WE BECOME DEERSTALKERS

Dennys and Robin and I together grew to enjoy the bush, and do a lot of the things that boys do in search of fun and adventure. Dennys and Robin are identical twins and there were times in their growing up years that even my family couldn't tell which was which. To me their thin and wiry frames, wavy black hair, and open and encouraging dispositions were, and still are, precious and enhancing factors in my life. Ross, who I will speak of later, was their father. We had bought bows and arrows and hunted anything that moved on the farms in the area that we lived. We had even got lucky at times and managed to shoot magpies, pukekos, eels, rabbits, hares, possums, ducks, and even a sparrow with the 20 to 30 pound bows that we had. We graduated to slug guns, and learnt to shoot fairly well with them, hitting tiny targets that we set up in the trees and tins that we'd throw into the air. Many birds fell to the slug guns too, and I'm afraid that we weren't very responsible with our selection at times. Finally, twenty twos were in our hands, and, from there, it wasn't long till we had high power rifles, and our legs took us into the real hunting country, deer country.

After I had found the Punga Hut, this became our destination almost every weekend during the last few years of school. In the last three years of high school, I spent over three hundred days in the hills according to my logbooks of those times. No wonder the headmaster of the high school told my friends not to associate with me, as he believed I was a bad influence on them. We thought that was a bit if a joke.

I had, from the beginning, written up all the trips that I had done into the hills and included photos of ourselves and the places we went to. Those books became very valuable in the years to come. We began to name all the ridges and clearings around Miro Valley, where the Punga Hut was situated, and I can still walk many of the bush tracks, purely in my mind, that we frequented so long ago. I can see the individual trees and walk around the corners in the tracks, seeing the next section as clear as day. It is a wonderful way to get to sleep when sleep is slow to come, in the early hours of the morning. Some of the places I never went back to for fifteen and twenty years, yet could still see them. What a surprise and a disappointment it was to go back after so long and not be able to find some of those tracks again. The trees and undergrowth of my memories had grown and didn't look the same anymore. You don't realize that the bush grows and changes until many years have passed. Some of the clearings that were so fruitful for deer have become choked up with scrub, and now are an effort to get through. I sometimes think that a match or two wouldn't go astray. However, that would be irresponsible wouldn't it?

The next poem I have included is a reminder of how inexperienced we were in those days, but also of the joys of our early hunting days. You don't have to be good at a thing to get a buzz from it. In fact, I wonder if becoming good at a thing spoils the enjoyment of it. When competitiveness comes in, the pure motives that we may have for doing a thing can be lost forever. Hunters can be terribly competitive as the story telling around a campfire or in a hunter's supplies shop testifies. What is the point of scoring trophies? Beautiful and desirable as antlers are, they are firstly a symbol of a living experience or an experience of living, and that can't be compared to another's experience. Certainly the size or proportions of the antlers give no comparative evaluation of the value of the hunter's experience in attaining them. Hunting is not about competitiveness.

What is it about hunting that grabs us? At the end of the day is it the antlers that you get? Yes, but it is more isn't it? Would the antlers be as valuable if you didn't have the scratched legs as well? Can you have a true hunting experience without cooking over the campfire? If the food tasted the same as back at home would you enjoy it as much? Would it be the same if you didn't work up a sweat and get really tired? Would it be the same if your feet never got wet or it never rained? Stumbling back to camp in the dark. Falling into the river at the last crossing. The sound of rain on the tent. The wonderful feeling of walking up a likely stream in the drizzling rain. The sound of wind blasting up the valley like a train, in gusts moving at a hundred miles an hour. The sharp feel of cold water running down your boots after you haven't crossed the river for some time. The weight of a good rifle in your hands with which you know you can hit anything within three hundred yards, and, if its close enough, even if it runs you will probably not miss. Even the mosquitoes and sand flies can add something. What am I saying? But isn't it true? Hunting isn't about antlers. It's not even about shooting. It's not even about photos. To me it's about wilderness. It's about being there. It's about the air that you breathe in the hills that seems to expand your lungs and your heart. It's about the wonderful expansive views that touch the unknown in all directions, and the "elbow room" that Davy Crockett spoke of. It's about the wonderful feeling of isolation and the need for self-reliant proficiency that is thrust upon you. It's about the danger of moving and living in rugged and uncertain terrain. It is all summed up in the feelings that you have, and the way that the wilderness affects you. Nothing is more exciting than being close to a wild animal in the wilderness. Shooting a deer on the bush edge of a farm, or on the edge of a road in a pine plantation is just not fully it, is it?

Somehow you're a different person while in the mountains, and I think that you're more who you really are then than any other time. That's what makes a hunter a hunter, and that is what makes a hunting experience valuable- the extent to which you experience wilderness. Some of my most exciting hunting adventures have culminated in the shooting of a yearling, and the biggest stag that I ever shot was one of the most ho-hum affairs. Now I look back on those days, when we were as green as frogs, with probably more nostalgic enjoyment than later on, when experience grew and successes were surer. Somehow there is a greater purity of enjoyment when we expect nothing and attempt everything. There was no failure for us when we took every success as a bonus. There is a lot of joy for those who are exploring a new thing in their lives, but when we start assessing our performance too much of that joy can be diminished.

The same principle showed when I played table tennis seriously as a teenager. When I was learning, I got a real buzz when I managed to pull off a tricky technique. But, when I had done it many times it didn't give so much enjoyment. I started to expect to do difficult things and so had negative enjoyment when I missed that practiced shot. And so, the thing that I started to do for fun became a thing that I competed against myself at by trying to do better or as well as yesterday, and the purity of playing for fun was compromised. Failure, which wasn't there in the beginning, entered into the whole experience as I became more proficient. I failed more in the beginning, but was only conscious of the successes. Later, I succeeded more, but was more conscious of the failures.

Being green can be a lot more fun in any endeavour. If your enjoyment of the hills revolves around securing antlers or bringing home the meat, then, in my opinion, you will eventually lose the pure enjoyment of hunting. If on the other hand your enjoyment of the hills revolves around being there in the wilderness, and experiencing whatever it dishes out, you can hold onto the pure joy and fun that it gave you when you first began. It's worth holding onto.

This poem is definitely about some green hunters. Many of us would be ashamed to have fired so many shots and scored so many misses in a few hours of hunting. Yet the last line reveals that all the failures were more than compensated for by one lucky success.

GREEN

Early one morning on a leather jacket choked ridge
Miro Valley spread out at our feet,
Three young friends climbed together to the top of a ledge
In cool sunlight, on a rock found a seat.
Field glasses to eyes, all the landscape we scanned
To find red deer in this rugged bush land.

At Home in the Hills

Then far to the south several ridges away
In a clearing on the top of a knob
A hind browsed, look below, another one lay,
And the blood in our veins 'gan to throb.
We selected a route through the scrubby terrain
A leatherjacket struggle and strain.

But the noise of our struggles was by other ears heard
And three hinds just nearby broke and ran.
Three shots up the ridge, they were really disturbed
But all missed, there was a lot still to learn.
Well the first deer we'd seen were still in their place
So we battled on at a slow noisy pace.

Then again, two deer, two, three hundred yards away
Feeding quietly on a rubbishy steep face.
A small war went off in that valley that day
But of venison we gained not a trace.
Yet nearer now to the first deer we'd seen
So we continued to - - - where they had been?

Shh, Just over this rise, and three young heads
Rose slowly and peered over the crest.
There's one, there's the other, the air again full of lead.
Amazing one was hit hard in the chest.
The dead one so scrawny we called it "the rat",
But how proudly on that high perch we sat.

The Green Novice

Robin Smith and the author (on the left). "The Rocks" (1969).

Chapter Four
Ross, a True Friend

First Hunt with Ross

I arrived home on the bus from high school one Friday afternoon, immediately changed into my jeans and sandshoes, untied my dog - a kelpie crossed with the best of twenty nine other breeds - and meandered off down the country road from our home, free. Free from schoolwork and uniform, homework expectations, and the claustrophobic city of Palmerston North where I attended school, for two wonderful days of the weekend. My dog 'Lucky' raced off and explored the long grass of the quiet country road I arrived ahead, as I sauntered along loving the freedom of being under the broad and ever changing sky. In the city now I miss the sky. It's still there but somehow you don't notice it as much in the city. I have always loved the sky, and at that time of my life used to spend hours lying on my back watching the clouds go over. The hawks were ever a fascination, circling against the blue and white above and seldom seeming to land.

It was my usual routine after school to take off into the farmland with my dog and simply roam. I did reasonably well at school, but the consistent comments from many teachers that more effort would give better results weren't without foundation. The farms

At Home in the Hills

within a five mile radius of my home were well known to me, and even the land of the farmer that didn't like me roaming his place was better known by me than him, as I sometimes had to prove when he came along. A boy finds all the little nooks and crannies inside drains and amongst bulrushes in swamps that an adult would never even look for.

So here I was, wandering down the one way sealed road, with Lucky searching the long grass beside it, when Ross Smith pulled up beside me. He is Dennys and Robin's father. "Want to go over to the Punga Hut?" he said. "I've already asked your parents and they said that it's O.K.". So I piled into the car. On the way back to my home to get my gear Ross pointed out a new rifle that he had in the back seat. It was a BSA monarch in 308 caliber. It looked so small that I thought that it was a twenty two until I looked at the bolt properly. Ross had never been to the Punga Hut and I don't know if I was invited along because I knew the way, or if I was genuinely wanted for my arresting company and hunting brilliance. As Ross was much older than I and had grown up in the high country of the South Island, I had to rule out the last two.

We picked up Ross's friend Bruce Rix, a tall local farmer topped with a mop of red hair, and arrived at the bush edge in Ross's short wheel based Landrover pickup, still sporting most of its army green coat. With less than two hours to get to the hut we wasted no time in packing our packs, and the pace to the top of the first ridge was set in top gear. I still hadn't really got to grips with the best way down into Miro Valley at that time, so we bush bashed it all the way arriving at the hut just before dark, and settled in for a comfortable night in anticipation of an early start.

Dawn found us fed and heading out of the hut for the ridge behind it where I had shot my first few deer. The clearings that were under the leatherjacket and interspersed erratically along the ridges were becoming familiar to me. As we made our way along a particular rocky, steeply dropping ridge, suddenly we saw a hind feeding about a hundred and fifty yards away across a gully in one of the clearings. At Bruce's hissed whisper to get down, we ducked behind a rocky outcrop on the open ridge. As she was looking straight at us I thought that this was a bit superfluous. However, the hind wasn't spooked due to the low hunting pressure that was common there then, and, after a minute or so I wondered what the guys were waiting for. I was the youngster and felt to follow the lead of the other two. As Bruce was the only one with a scope sight I finally, impatiently, suggested that he shoot. After some shuffling of his body and poking of his rifle over the rocks, interspersed with whispering and grunting, he fired, and to my utter astonishment nothing happened. How could he miss? So Ross fired. Still the hind didn't move. I remember thinking, "For goodness sake it won't stay there all day, I may as well shoot it." I fired and the hind crumpled to the ground about my fifth or sixth deer. I felt a bit funny shooting it after two grown and experienced men had tried and missed. It was a bit of a quandary.

Ross soon saw the movement of another deer in another clump of leatherjacket higher up the ridge and fired. I didn't even see what he had shot at but he said that it had fallen. We clambered down into the gutty creek clogged with all manner of impassable shrubs, then scraped our way up through the inhospitable leatherjacket to the deer that I had shot, and found that, as well as my shot in its shoulder, it had another bullet hole through its right ear. Ross then said that he had aimed at its head so we assumed that that was his shot. Obviously Bruce's rifle was not shot in for the scope that he had it mounted with, and the fate of his shot was anybody's guess.

We lost another deer to an attempted headshot of Ross' some years later when he and I were fencing together. We could have done with the money at the time too. It was a rainy day and was obviously too wet to work, so we went hunting and got thoroughly saturated. I usually keep head shots for times when you can't see any other part of the deer, however, I do remember that there was a time when I had a run of head shots. Got nine stags in a row over several days, all shot in the head. That though was when I was meat hunting some years later.

Ross and Bruce boned out the two carcasses and I learned how to do it another way quite different from my first attempt. It was probably the right way to do it and I have adopted it myself now. My load wasn't boned out till back at the hut and consisted of two hind legs still connected together with the skin over the spine. Wrapped around my waist and tied together in front with a piece of bailing twine so that the weight rested on my hips didn't make a very comfortable load. Getting through leatherjacket is hard enough, but with this extra load pinching against my waist........ Well, it wasn't comfortable and I've never carried meat like that since. I was glad to get back to the hut for breakfast.

There are many stories that I could tell about Ross. Like the time I was wagging school and walking the slow way to Fitzherbert Ave. from my high school in Featherston St. My route went via Longburn, Linton Army Camp and Aukautere and I came across Ross putting up a fence on the side of Old West road. He made no comment as I walked up to him. I would have dodged him if I had seen him before he saw me.

As he straightened his back, easing the muscles after clanging staples into the lower wires on the row of neatly spaced battens stretching out behind him, he simply said to me, "Can you do with a cup of tea?" We sat there on clumps of long grass beside the road together, eating his sandwiches without a word of why I wasn't at school and what was I doing on Old West Rd. While he smoked the ever present wrinkled home made, miraculously clinging to his bottom lip, we talked a little between long silences of comradeship. Ross and I were from different generations and were different in so many ways, but there was something alike in us that I have never been able to really isolate - it's not important that I do, for we were what we were to each other, and we both enjoyed it. I found out in later years from him that he had missed a lot of school, much more than I, when he was young, and didn't need to ask what I was doing. He was a great guy Ross.

STAG ON THE BACK RIDGE

Another time we were hunting together along a ridge that was strewn with clearings amongst five to ten foot rubbishy scrub. His short hair, twenty years out of fashion, appeared and disappeared between the bushes as we made our way along. We poked our heads out of the pepperwood and stuff that grew just below the leatherjacket into a clearing that was so small that it didn't really deserve the dignity of the name. One of an endless number that dotted the ridge and that we had found some relief in during the morning. I began to survey some clearings on a distant ridge through the scope on my rifle while I assumed that Ross was doing the same.

I spoke and was answered with a sharp "Shhh". Ross was attentive to the scrub just in front of us! Then I heard what had got his attention. A deer was feeding only a few yards from the clearing below us on the ridge face. We slowly craned our necks this way and that, aware of the need to make no noise, but couldn't see over or around the thick scrub. Ross climbed onto a stumpy relic of a rotting tree but still couldn't get a sight of the tantalizing animal that was feeding, oblivious to us, off the twigs just in front. Slowly, I lay down and began to poke my rifle about, parting the leaves at ground level. There he was - about ten feet in front of me. Easing the bolt down on my rifle, I found

At Home in the Hills

that I couldn't get my face low enough to see through the scope. I could see part of the shoulder and the small branches that were being tugged as he picked the leaves from them. Pointing the rifle without the aid of sights I fired and he was down.

Using the front lower legs for cleverly cut toggles and inserting them through the back legs, Ross put the stag on his back and lead us off down through that densely scrubbed ridge. As I carried both rifles, I mostly followed the sound of Ross as he leaned and pushed his way down through the bushes until the trees gained height, and we were able to walk underneath and see each other. I had all my work cut out for me just keeping up with him. Ross was known by those who had been with him in the bush as a bit of a mountain goat. Tough, wiry and fit. He sure showed me that day what a man of forty can do that a teenager can't. Above all Ross was a great guy. A real mate. A person to be like. And he had eyes like a hawk. Literally.

One day we were sitting in a clearing, on a ridge up Quartz creek, where we had been hunting since daybreak. We were having lunch and dreamily gazing out over the creek far below with a distant bush clad ridge over against us, about a thousand yards away. We had the meat of a hind that I'd shot an hour earlier in our packs and were on the point of heading for home.

After we had been sitting there for some time Ross asked me to get my binoculars out of my pack because he said he could see four deer over on the ridge face one thousand yards away. There were no clearings on that bush clad ridge face but I never argued with Ross. He wasn't always right but he was always a nice bloke, and I say without hesitation that I loved him. So he guided my binocular enhanced vision into the things he could see on that ridge. It's always a challenge to guide someone into seeing the same thing that you're looking at over distance in the hills. It's done something like this: See that big dead stump below the skyline where that fluffy wisp of a cloud is? Well come directly down about a finger length and you'll see a large Rimu sticking up out of the bush. Yeah, the big one to the left of the smaller one. Well go about fifty yards to the left of that to where you can see a small dark spot, and just above that there is a light green punga with the sun on it. Look just to the left of that and there is a deer under a small bank-like thing there. See it? I was astonished after listening to Ross guide me like this, to find that two of the things that he could see, were deer. The other two were dead punga fronds. How he had picked up those animals in thick bush at that distance I don't know.

Without the binoculars I could barely make out the color of the animals, and I know that even now at forty six my eyes are excellent. Recent testing told me that I would pass commercial pilot's requirements for eyesight at the highest level, for a person less than half my age. But Ross' eyesight left mine for dead.

Another time we were hunting on a ridge in the Tokomaru River and had again stopped for a look around, and for Ross to have a go at his tobacco tin. I was glassing the slips and clearings across the way when Ross said, "Just before we go would you look at that slip up there and tell me there's no deer on it".

Way up the valley, in between the Ngawakarara and Mairekau peaks, was a slip in the creek at what seemed to be about a mile beyond the country that should be interesting us at that moment. I glanced at the slip with the binoculars and blow me down if there wasn't a stag beneath a punga right in the middle of that slip. I said aloud and with amazement, "There is one there!" When I looked at Ross he had a look on his face that wasn't a smile and yet was full of amusement, a twinkle in his eye, and I realized that he had been watching that stag for some time while puffing on the wrinkled strand of cigarette paper that he called a smoke. Ross had good eyes and I think that I have only come across one other that came near to it. It must be handy to have biological ten-power vision.

There was the time that we were opossum trapping and poisoning together on a long bush edge above the Kahuterawa stream. Our traps and baits were strung out dodging in and out of where tongues of bush reached up into the farm land from the tangle of kie kie and other impossible scrub in the very steep and bluff ridden slopes below. An opossum haven. However they were drawn to a crop of turnips only a few paddocks away and their paths were well trodden through the long grass on the ridges coming out of the fenced off bush where cattle and sheep may not be found.

This particular August was not unlike all others in that area. At an altitude of about a thousand feet these hills were the first to force upward the winter winds and their load of rain-laden clouds after their trip over the Tasman Sea. The ground was always sodden, the wind always seemed to be blowing and we were always wrapped in wool and lace up gumboots. Some of the frozen possum carcasses were hard to skin as fingers that were fighting to keep circulation going lost the bout.

There was a flu going about that was commonly known as the Hong Kong flu and Ross and I both got it. The lines were harder to reach and follow, as we were both depleted in energy. However we couldn't leave our lines as we were operating about one hundred and twenty traps and the thought of a possum having to be in one for two days was beyond our idea of decency. We tried every type of cough mixture on the shelves of the chemists finally settling on Buckleys Canadiol Mixture. It seemed to be the only one that could move that nagging tickle in the throat that forced you to cough and cough and cough. When one of us was caught in a coughing fit the other would take out the bottle of burning stuff, pour out a capful of it, and, between coughs, throw it down the others throat. We drank it quite freely in this manner. One time however, we both got the coughs at the same time. It was a bad attack for both of us. Neither of us could get the bottle out as we were fully involved in body wracking, foot stamping, jumping up and down coughing finally being humbled to elbows and knees on the ground barking into the hillside. I recovered first and rolled over onto the ground exhausted. Soon Ross did the same and then we did the wrong thing. We looked at each other. The ridiculousness of our situation occurred to us both at the same time and we started laughing. And laughing. Rolling around the hillside laughing. Helpless arm waving laughing that multiplied each time we looked at each other. Where we got the energy for it I don't know as we had been wrung out from the preceding coughing.

It was a major comedown to have to get up shortly after and plod off along the long, familiar, twisting line of traps, poison baits and dead opossums waiting to be skinned, but we did it with a lightness of step and heart that punctuated much of our time together.

Ross died a few years back. Tears still come to my eyes when I think of him. He was what we call now, a role model for me as I grew up, but he was more than that too. He was a friend of the highest order and yet more than that. This says it better. He was…

…A R EAL F RIEND

He talked about me all the time she said.
And now it's hard to understand he's dead.
No one understood me more than he,
And I understood that which was his heart.

At Home in the Hills

> *Others knew the bush and we'd both shared*
> *Those times with them upon the hill.*
> *But to us the mountains were no pastime or sport,*
> *They filled our souls, and fill mine still.*

> *"He loved me," now they say.*
> *But oh what he has meant to me.*
> *He knew the home of a bend in a creek,*
> *And the friendliness of a crown fern glade.*
> *He would light a fire and boil a brew,*
> *Warm a winters storm and my storm too.*

> *I never thought he'd die.*
> *I thought he'd see me to my grave.*
> *Not a big man, he didn't say much.*
> *Yet to me he seemed as strong as the earth.*
> *He was there, always there. And now,*
> *He's gone.*
> *Oh Ross....*

This is another poem that speaks of Ross and reveals something of what we experienced and what he meant, and still means to me. I couldn't leave it out.

Ross

> *We trapped 'possums together one winter.*
> *Trod the hills skinning hundreds of them.*
> *The rain, mud and frost made it harder,*
> *But his company turned boys into men.*

Ross, a True Friend

We hunted deer and lugged them to sale
From the far bush clad hills that we knew.
Heavy loads but our backs didn't fail
And our friendship in leaps and bounds grew.

We worked the farm ridges out back
Where sun tanned and where freezing winds blew.
Fencing the land with a knack
That he'd taught me the last month or two.

I was young and he had sons my age,
But it seemed we were equals and mates,
For we both measured to the same gauge
Where the mountains and valleys give rates.

He's gone now but I can still see
The twinkle the bush brought to his eye.
The way that his shoulders swung free
And the love that he had for me.

Ross was a man. He worked dawn to dark most days of his life. As a high country musterer when he was younger, then shearer, fencer, possum trapper, farm worker of all kinds. He was a husband, a father (of my closest friends). He was weather beaten in his features and carried the quiet way of all who have had their life in the open. He spoke to you eye to eye, yet not as the city folk do from an unsettling distance of two or three feet - from the country perspective of ten to twenty feet so that you have room to breathe.

He wore the uniform of the country. Black woolen singlet. Woolen shearer's longs, or cotton khaki shorts. Checked woolen shirt. Lace up gumboots over woolen socks. He accepted his friends without criticism, and never talked of another if he didn't

At Home in the Hills

have something good to say about them. A smile from him meant more than the many words of another you had impressed. Although he worried about money, a good portion of his life trying to make ends meet, he was not interested in accumulating it for its own sake. He inspired me to write this poem too.

LITTLE MEN AND BIG MEN

The sun shines down on both the town
And distant mountain places,
And I have seen them both up close,
I've seen all of their faces.

The town has streets with earth beneath,
I think it's suffocated.
The air bequests a million breaths
Of those who've exhalated.

Ten thousand trucks and cars all chuck
Their fumes upon the street,
That air condition each partition
Of offices of, the elite?

The people scrawny in a hurry
Splashed with colours bright,
Swarm the place as if to race
Each other at the lights.

And rusty hulks of ships with bulks
Of goods from distant lands
Leak oil and slime out all the time

Ross, a True Friend

That slug the local sands.

But when it's night and all the lights
Come on in glorious points,
The people go to smoky shows,
Get drunk in all the joints.

The mountains are different by far
With rock and plant and tree.
Air that's clean can make, it seems,
A soul feel young and free.

The mountain water can be sought for
Drink so bright and clear.
The slopes will make your limbs to take
On vigorous healthy cheer.

There's naught to prove and room to move
At a pace that just suits you.
And where before you've been there's more
To see and more to do.

Folks alas aren't seen in mass
But each met eye to eye.
And honest men are the best friends
In land that's do or die.

The rain is pure, the winds a cure
To those with inner haste.
And if snowbound peace can be found
Where clocks and calendars waste.

At Home in the Hills

> *Have you my friend seen little men*
> *In streets who chase the dollar?*
> *I choose the giant man who stands*
> *Alone by camp and fire.*

Chapter Five
Eels, Cowpies and Off-centre Things

Stag Ride

I rose an hour or so before dawn and had been driving on the one way, metaled, Kahuterawa Road towards the Black Bridge for some time before the feeling of being up in the middle of the night left and my head cleared. Here the Kahuterawa River leaves the Road and travels on its own, eastward, and into the closeness of steep hills towards the peak called Baldy. About an hour of easy and enjoyable walking up the small but beautiful river, a tributary called Quartz Creek suddenly and inconspicuously slips into the main flow of the Kahuterawa river from behind a deceptive boulder on the true right, and it is here that I was headed.

The main river, where I often stopped for a refreshing, but always-cold swim, alternated from smooth shingle banks siding deep green pools, to deep and coldly shaded gorges which had their secrets to negotiate. Just as I rounded the last bend bringing me into sight of the forks, I spotted two stags in the river itself, wading up to their bellies, about a hundred yards ahead of me. The splashing of their movement through the water flicking into the air highly visible droplets of clear northern Tararua liquid, silhouetted against the darkness of the shaded rocky backdrop, was the first thing to catch my eye. They were moving in a lazy fashion, in no hurry to climb out of the bouldery rapids, where they had obviously, but unusually, spent the last few hours, to a suitable camp for the heat of the day that was not far away.

Finding a suitable rock and bending at an awkward angle in knee deep water behind it, I soon had the larger of them in the field of my Pecar scope and one hundred and fifty grains of lead was on its way. An eight point stag in the velvet. The other stag just seemed to evaporate from the river and where he went was a mystery. Amazing how deer can do that. Also amazing how they can run through solid bush.

At another time, while following a track in secondary growth bush that I was hunting, and on rounding a bend in it, a hind suddenly lifted her head up thirty yards in front of me. The look on her face was that one that states pretty clearly that she is no doubt what you are and what you have in mind concerning her future, and, in less time than it takes for you to realize that a billy handle is too hot to be holding, she was flying out of sight, off the narrow blazed track. My rifle didn't even twitch in my hands she was gone so quick.

Her disappearance was followed by an incredible crashing and smashing of twigs and leaves, clunking of logs, and rattling of rocks as I approached her departure point with interest. I knew that this was a hind that there would be no point in tracking. Where she had left the track was not a place I would have chosen to go. It was a solid wall of pepperwood jutting out of large, greasy surfaced, rotting logs lying all over each other, and all this wrapped in a curtain of falling bushlawyer descending from a pair of Miro trees that were in the process of being strangled by their unwanted attacker.

Eels, Cowpies and Off-centre Things

I parted the branches a little with my rifle barrel to see if I could find just which six-inch square of opening the hind had disappeared into. This only revealed an even deeper and more tangled interior to that particular piece of over indulged mess. And that hind had leapt into and run through there. Amazing.

Another time, carrying a small stag on my pack frame over a high bush ridge, enroute to the bank in town, I twisted my way through a clump of pepperwood scrub about eight feet in height, making visibility only one or two feet. Levering the legs and neck of the deer off unknown things behind my back - that interminably frustrates anyone carrying an animal like that - I burst into a small shaded clearing. Suddenly, from under my feet, literally, a hind leapt up from where she must have been dozing until I broke in on her bedroom, crossed the clearing in a flash, and, as it was bounded by similar scrub as that that I had entered this tiny intimate place through, exited the only way showing a visible gap and was gone. However, the nature of that gap is worth noting.

At the other side of the clear spot was a log about five feet in diameter, lying sideways, supported about two feet off the ground by one of a number of barkless branches protruding from its trunk. The only way over the log was between more branches, which left only one large enough gap about eight feet above the ground. The hind didn't even notice that possibility. Running at full speed, which she had attained in a body length, such was her repulsion of me; she dropped onto her belly and ran through the two-foot gap under the log. Legs and hooves went everywhere like a dozen samurai swords attacking a fly. A second later she was gone. After my bottom jaw had slowly climbed back into position, I set about the task of following her. It took me about three minutes to negotiate that log with my load. Again, amazing.

Well, back to my stags in the river. That second one disappeared from a gorgy length of it, to, I don't know where. However, turning to the one lying in the water and as it was still early, I decided to attempt to get this deer whole out to the Black Bridge. I had no pack frame to carry it on and I was not strong enough to do that anyway. It was a large-bodied stag and I couldn't lift it at all. The only way was to try to float it down in the water. So began a saga that lives in my memory well.

It was beginning to be the sunny day that the stars before daybreak had promised, and, as it was summer I enjoyed a great time wading and splashing along with my stag. It glided easily enough in the sparkling water and needed little effort to pull over the shallower places, where the smooth rocks were showing through the surface. Holding onto the velvet antlers was comfortable and smooth and I was enjoying the walk. A hunter in the beautiful wild of a backcountry river with his quarry successfully gained.

At one point though, while dragging it down the river by the antlers, I came to an eight-foot waterfall. I casually walked out onto the top of it in knee-deep water over a shingle base to see how I could get the deer carcass down it. It was the kind of waterfall that is made from a huge fallen tree that had got itself jammed between the extreme banks of the river, in some massive flood in times past. Then the stones had rolled up to it and become jammed against it in successive floods until all the gaps had been plugged up with fine shingle and silt, and the whole stream above the original tree trunk was flat and raised to its upper height. Now the water was pouring over the log in a sheet that spread along much of its length.

As I walked into the sharply angling sun, the insects dancing above the water downstream, brightly sunlit like tiny mirrors in the haze in front of me must have had a hypnotizing effect. Forgetting that the current was carrying the deer forward by itself I walked right to the edge of the waterfall and stopped to look over. The carcass didn't stop and, powered by the current, caught me behind the knees landing me sitting on its ribcage, and taking me with it, unwittingly, over the fall into the deep pool below. There have been many times in the hills that I wish I had had a camera and there have been as many times that I have been glad that no one has had a camera. This was one of those times but I'm not sure which one.

It is the only deer that has ever given me a ride anywhere, and, if that's typical of the kinds of rides that deer give, then we're better to stick to horses. Lucky it was a hot day and the dousing did me good, and I got a laugh out of it. One minute standing in the sunshine, warm and dry, enjoying the bush and the music of the stream on a dreamy day. The next minute, a metre under water in a cold, greenish tinted, deep pool, being pulled under further by a rifle in one hand, a stag's antler in the other and heavy leather boots on wildly flapping feet. I disappeared from daylight momentarily. With a wild flapping of hands and adrenaline enhanced kicking of feet I managed to stop either my rifle or the stag from sinking six metres to the bottom of the pool, and a heavy, exhausted and embarrassed hunter hauled himself to the edge.

Some things you do in the hills are so embarrassing that you look around to see if anyone saw that. Even knowing that you're alone you still look about. Like the time when I was culling out of Maropea Forks hut and in the middle of the day found a really nice warm slip covered in three foot long grasses, weeds and shrubs, interspersed with short cropped clear spots. As I had been in the cool of the bush for some time and was also aware that bush hunting doesn't do your suntan much good, I decided to strip off my shirt and lie down for a bit and get some sunbathing done. However I fell asleep.

I don't know if he had been there all the time or if he arrived after I fell asleep, however he was as unaware of my presence where he was sleeping nearby as I was of his. Finally, I slowly emerged out of the heavy and heady murk of a midday sleep in the direct heat and glare of the sun. If you know what that is like you will know the dry mouth and generally ill feeling that fuzzes your mind and slows you joints down, together making a pathetically pitiful human being fit for little good for a time. Slowly, I wavered to my feet and through bleary eyes squinted about. He must have heard me as the next thing that I was aware of was the frightened eyes and twisting velvet antlers of a four point stag about thirty feet in front of me rising from where it had been bedded down sunbathing too. My rifle lay on the ground two meters away, and, as I in seemingly slow motion reached for it, the stag, in what seemed like sped up motion, left, bounding off across the slip and into the trees unmolested. I stood there like an idiot. Then I did it. I looked around to see if anyone had been watching. Why do we do that? We haven't seen anyone for hours or perhaps days in some cases, and yet we look to see if anyone saw us. Hangover from teasing that we have received sometime in our childhood I suppose.

As I approached the hut that night I wondered where Chris Satherley, my culling mate, had been hunting that day. I figured that if he had been on the opposing ridge from me and had seen me I would just say that I had been lying down with the stag, plying him for inside information on the habits of deer and where the others of his clan were hanging out. Having to make up an excuse for it shows how embarrassed I'd felt.

Back to my story again. Having survived the waterfall I carried on down the river, wet through and tiring when I came to a deep hole where I had to push the deer around the face of a big rock, let it go, run around the rock to the other side, and grab the deer again before it sunk into the hole. I managed it all successfully and had grabbed the antlers before the stag had sunk into the depths. But as I was pulling it to the stony ledge again I noticed a huge eel probing the open stomach area of the animal that I was hoping would pay my keep for the next week. He wasn't going to have it. I stood above the deer and aimed my rifle at the freeloader's substantial front end, which was about five feet from the back end and a foot below the surface of the clear water. It was a one hundred and seventy five grain seven by fifty seven projectile that hit the water directly above that eels head. I never saw what happened to the eel. Did you know that when you fire a high power bullet into the water like that a jet of water comes back up the line of the bullet at a tremendous rate of knots? It hit my face so hard that some of it drove up behind my eyelids quite painfully.

By the time that I could see again, after much blind groping around to find a safe place to put my rifle, secure the deer and then clean my eyes out, the eel was gone - either dead at the bottom of the deep green hole or cowering in quivering amazement in some crevice of the river. Seeing that seven by fifty sevens have been successfully used to hunt elephants by some of the old Great White Hunters of the nineteenth century, I somehow think that it would hardly be the latter.

I finally got the deer to market carrying it through Palmerston North, draped along the front mudguard of my friend's nineteen thirty eight Plymouth with the antlers tied to the front bumper, creating quite a stir amongst the citified onlookers along the way.

EELS AND COWPIES

A few years later, while deerstalking with Robin, we saw an eel in a pool of a small creek. It took some talking to get him to shoot it with his three oh eight. When he'd cleaned the water out of his eyes and I had got up from the ground where I had been rolling around laughing, we found the eel in the bottom of the pool unmoved and quite dead. I suspect that that bigger eel a few years earlier had died too.

Its funny how that works. Bullets hitting liquid, or soft stuff close to being liquid, can send that jet of the soft stuff back at the rifle. Some years earlier, and I should have learnt from this, Dennys, Robin and I had been amusing ourselves with twenty twos, magpies and rabbits etc. It was a spring day and we were walking through a paddock recently vacated by a herd of milking cows. The grass was all chewed down to the rough stalks and the whole field had nice wet, green cowpies all over the place. I don't know whose idea it was, though I have my suspicions and I'm sure that you have too, but as one of my friends that were with me walked by a particularly big cowpie a twenty two bullet, from an undisclosed source, hit it. The spray splattered all over the flabbergasted victim from head to foot. What can you say? Well actually I didn't say much but he was only short of something to say for about thirty seconds with that look that a cat has when you take away his food plate - total unbelieving indignation. Then he said quite a bit, as I remember, and we were in no doubt as to his feelings about the incident either.

A little bit further on as we continued through the paddock the victim thought that he would get his own back and so surreptitiously dropped behind us others. The next thing, 'Bang'! Unfortunately the angle must have been different the second time, for instead of projecting the green stuff forward as I.... I mean, as had happened the first time, the principle of the eels in the creek had operated, and the original victim had again been splattered as the green substance had returned back up the line of his bullet. With hands hanging dejectedly at his side, and shoulders drooping, the look of defeat on his muck splotched face was priceless.

Eels, Cowpies and Off-centre Things

I'm sure that some of you would think that this was an irresponsible act. Those of you who don't think it was are wrong. But that was what happened and it sure was funny at the time.

I was brought up with three basic rules about rifles and to those I have added a few. They are:

1) Never touch any rifle unless you have the owners express permission. Whenever picking up any rifle immediately open the bolt regardless of whether or not you believe it is loaded.
3) Never aim a rifle or allow the barrel of a rifle to pass across the line of a person.
4) Never have a loaded rifle within fifty yards of a camp or hut.
5) Never fire at anything that you cannot identify as the game you area after with one hundred percent certainty.

I have never shot at anything that I wasn't absolutely, one hundred per cent sure of. I have had shots go past me though on two occasions, one of which, I am sure was aimed at me or a movement that I had made. The next chapter tells the stories of those two times.

CHAPTER SIX
Stray Bullets, Stray People

❦

I was just eighteen by a few days before that April day in nineteen sixty-eight, and had a few weeks off work for the roar. I was picking my way down a waterlogged leatherjacket and scrub strewn ridge off a small peak called Scrub keeping my eyes sweeping the thick waist to shoulder high scratchy growth ahead as I went, looking for the deep red blaze of a deer amidst the darkness of the tangled foliage.

The scrub has grown overhead height now and the name of the peak has become more apt in later years. It was one of those dark and drizzly days which seem to be almost minutes away from nightfall all the time. Cloud cover was just a hundred feet or so over my head and hung there with an ominous heaviness. There were small wisps of cloud winding up the valleys and the higher up side creeks way over towards Ngawakarara high point and further south towards Mairekau, its partner, and hovering below me in the Tokomaru River and further south.

It was a Monday and I had been out of the bush at home for the night after a fruitless few days in the area with a friend. He had

At Home in the Hills

to go back to work and I had headed back into the hills alone, where I was already feeling the quiet contentment as I fitted in with the pace. At some point on the ridge, as I ducked, dodged and sidled my way along, a reasonably loud roar emanated out of the valley immediately to the south, stopping me instantly in my tracks. I pulled the foot long cow horn, that always accompanies me during the season that the hills come alive with roaring stags, from beneath my gray oversized swanny jacket and moaned a reply as loud as my voice would allow.

I must have the right sort of voice for roaring stags as I've never had any trouble getting them to answer me. Others I know, better hunters than I, have no luck at all, and yet they sound like the real McCoy to me. I wasn't sure whether the stag off over the edge of the ridge would be able to hear me or not. I was facing directly into the southerly that was picking up (it kept on picking up too for the next few days and culminated in the sinking of a large ferry *Wahine* in Cook Strait).

Straight away an answering roar blew back at me on the wind causing the hair to prickle on the back of my neck. It got to be quite a lot of fun for the next few minutes. Roaring back and forth with a wild stag is a great experience. However, as the time went on I wasn't confident that the stag was making any headway in my direction. Then another stag began to roar directly over the stag that I was in conversation with, but on the next ridge south, about a mile away. Soon I could tell that the stag that I had been roaring was going away from me to the stag upwind from him, that he would be able to hear better, rather than me who was downwind.

I stopped roaring and began to move in their direction, hoping to close in on the two of them when they met. I was hoping to perhaps see two stags fighting, a sight that I still haven't seen. The bush was low and thick with undergrowth, especially crown fern, but I was used to it and didn't have much trouble getting through it quickly. After forty minutes or so it was getting to that point where I was treading softly, my boots seeking out the lumps of moss, areas of bare earth, and solid tree roots that would make no noise to betray my passage. I was peering around every tree ready to lower the bolt on my rifle as soon as I sighted the animal that must be only yards away. Both deer seemed to be so near. The trees were very close together there, and I realized that when I sighted one of them he would probably only be ten yards away at most. The hair on my neck was just beginning to stand up on my neck and every nerve and sense was tuned to a pitch.

Suddenly, "BOOM" - a shot blasted through the trees and my whole being, tense as it was, jerked within me. It was the last thing I was expecting and my heart stopped for a second while I received a few litres of adrenaline into my blood stream. My eyes leapt out in front of my eyebrows and back in a second, I'm sure, finally settling into a pale face, jolted with shock.

The shot must have come from little more than ten yards away from me under the spindly trees that clumped together there. I immediately surmised that the second stag that I had heard, and that my stag had preferred to approach, was in fact another hunter. I yelled out, "Did you get him"? The only answer was the usual stillness of the bush after a rifle discharge. I yelled it out louder. "Did you get him"? Still, to my surprise there was no answer. Why didn't the shooter answer? There was no doubt that he could hear me. He had to be no further than a few yards away. Then it struck me. There could only be one reason. The hunter had not seen the deer that he was shooting at but had only seen a movement - either mine or the stags - whichever, he wasn't sure which one it was. He had fired at a movement. When I yelled he realized his mistake, thought he may have fired at me, and so kept quiet.

A few minutes and several hundred yards later, way down the valley and under a ceiling of punga fronds covering a creek terrace, I stopped to take a breath. I had been moving on pure adrenaline, swinging along the slopes, dropping down and down, and taking the path that would cover the most ground as quickly as possible - and I was hopping mad. It took quite a while for my body to settle down. Slowing then, I ambled along for a half-hour or so to a clearing where my tent fly was erected, still standing where I had left it the previous day.

The morning drifted, as those damp days do prior to the arrival of a significant storm, and I occupied the time catching a billy full of fresh water crayfish, which I cooked over a smoky fire that struggled to stay alive amongst a huddle of damp and barely usable wood. By mid-afternoon I had worked the anger out of my system, and had stopped planning what I would do to that guy if he happened to walk into my campsite. I don't know how close that bullet came to ending my life there and then.

I saw another six deer in the following two days as the wind rose steadily, blowing up the creeks and through the bush flats, bending the punga fronds upward, exposing their white undersides, releasing a freshness that I enjoy being amongst. I remember having a lot of fun with two stags that roared well in the bush, seeming to always be just out of sight beyond the cast of my vision, but who bellowed at me as if they were going to rush up and do me in any second. One old campaigner fell to my rifle, though too tough to eat. His antlers finally found their way to the wall of a nearby hut. But I did manage to have venison for each meal those days due to a yearling that I spotted tip toeing away under the brush of the undergrowth with mistaken stealth.

The fourth day was the day the *Wahine* sunk and most New Zealanders were glad to be at home protected from the storm that lashed the country on those days. I awoke under the nylon tent fly after torrential rains and high winds in the night had flapped it around like a rag. I had been slipping out from under it the previous few nights owing to the slope that I had set camp up on, and the slippery grass that I had put under my sleeping bag to soften the effect of the cold ground. I never did have a decent sleeping bag.

I got up in the night, and with my tomahawk, sharpened and drove a stake into the ground to put my foot on while I slept, to stop me sliding out again and getting the sleeping bag wet in the rain. This did at least stop one foot from slipping out of the tent. I woke up many times in the night with one foot extended and the other knee up under my chin. Everything had slipped except that foot. It was still on the stake and my chin was resting on my knee, my whole leg asleep. It took me a while to wriggle myself, and the bag, back up into the tent fly properly and straighten my leg, now suffering the pins and needles, and feel the blood seep painfully back into it again. Then I turned over, put the other foot on the stake, and again fell asleep quickly. A few hours later the whole process would be repeated for the other leg.

The long days on my feet in difficult, thick bush added to the enjoyment of the storm's power, effectively sending me to sleep easily. I've always loved storms, especially when I am able to experience them from a dry spot, and have found falling asleep no problem in the noise and bluster. An hour or so later, pins and needles again and then the other leg's turn. It was a long night, as many nights in the bush can be, but I think that you get more sleep than you realize, even when you think that you were awake all night. At least, I've never felt excessively tired on the hill on days following those nights. Your body sleeps when you really need it.

The morning revealed that the creek, that was normally about three inches deep and could be walked through with ease not topping ankle boots, was brown, deep and pounding and unable to be waded through. Any attempt would have ended up in my being carried over the sixty foot waterfall just below and no doubt killed. So, I had to go the long way around, up into

At Home in the Hills

the headwaters of the creek, which were still only marginal for crossing, but, as the stream was running slower, I could cross, swim, wade through it.

I remember a very bewildered hind up on the raging ridge in the gale-driven cloud on the way out to the car. Deer are interesting to watch during really bad weather. It's an easy time to hunt too, as long as flooded streams don't slow you up or put paid to your plans.

One time I was high up on a ridge when a thunder and lightning storm came up the valley. Deer appeared everywhere. They just wandered out onto the open ridges in twos and threes, looking up and around the valley as if they were trying to work out what was happening. In the twenty minutes that the lightning was crashing about before the rain came in great drops of what seemed like half a cup each, every spot where you could see a deer in that valley had a couple in it. As the curtain of rain came they went just as quickly.

When I finally got home from that weekend of the Wahine storm, soaked and ready for a bath, I wasn't surprised to be told that a ship was in trouble in Cook Strait.

The other time that I came close to being shot was a few years later when I was culling in the North West Ruahines. Four of us had left the Mokai Base at the back of the Mokai Station heading for Ohutu Stream Hut. Three of us were to open up the track to Ohutu Ridge and the other was the illustrious government gun, alias the Mangaohane Man - known to his mother, my father's cousin, as Jim Warren. He was heading for the wonderful hunting country of the Aorangi bluffs and the Reporoa Bog, enroute to the Mangaohane and Otupae killing grounds. One of the others was a student laborer and the other was another Forestry hunter.

As we were walking the sidling track above Ohutu Stream a hundred feet or so above the water, we sighted four hinds on the big grassy clearings about a hundred yards away on the east side of the creek. We all settled in with our backs to the bank on the side of the track, with our various rifles loaded and ready, one deer allotted to each of us. Two, two four threes, one triple two and a thirty oh six. After a signal, and on the following silent count of three, we all fired. Two of the hinds fell dead on the spot from the two, two four threes, one ran, having been missed by the thirty oh six, and the one that I fired at with my triple two staggered away around a small ridge into one of many clumps of trees that strung out in a network over the whole face. She didn't come out and I knew from the shot that I had fired and the way she had reacted that she never would.

The triple two is a very effective calibre. I twice shot deer at over four hundred meters with mine and only ever lost two that I hit with it, both at close range. One was a large bodied stag on the sides of the Maropea River near the Mokai Base. The shot hit him fair and square in the ribs, and in two bounds he disappeared into a growth of giant stinging nettle covering acres of the hillside. There was no way that I was going in there though I knew that he was probably only yards away dead. A heavy calibre would most likely have dropped him on the spot and I would have had another tail that month.

The other one I lost survived. I had come across her just off the track below the peak Rongotea on the Mokai Patea Range. Being above her and about fifty yards away, I aimed just under her spine and although the shot was good she ran. I tracked her for some time, and, although I had found some hair from the shot, there was no blood and finally her tracks eluded me.

Some months later I was talking to Terry Lambert, who hunted on the block after me, and he told me about an unusual hind that he had shot on the sides of the Mokai Patea near Rongotea peak. He said he shot a hind that had a long scar along her back just under the spine. It had just passed from being a scab and had healed well. Sometimes the triple two has a tendency to explode on impact and not penetrate at all, and this was what had obviously happened in that case. A fawn that I shot on the run in the Tararuas was nearly cut in half with the same rifle a year or so later and it was then that I realized that I wanted another, slightly heavier calibre. That's when I came across the Sako two four three that did me so well and with which I secured many animals. I never lost one to that rifle. However I really liked the triple two and would like to own one again one day.

The only other deer that I know that I hit and lost was with a seven by fifty seven, but that's another story. Jim Warren soon after collected the tail from that one out in the Mangaohane tussock, and it was on its last legs when he shot it.

But this one on the Ohutu Stream sidings that ran unhurt was the one allotted to the student worker that was with us filling in his holidays. I guess it says something for the steady shooting of those who are not affected by too much excitement at the prospect of getting a deer. It seems, too, that often the person that has an accident shooting is the one who gets little opportunity to shoot, and when seeing the chance to get a deer can act too quickly or carelessly.

As it was only a few minutes walk along the benched track to the hut, I offered to go down the bank, over the creek and up into the clearings on the other side to get the tails and see if I could knock over the hind that ran, while the others went on to the hut and began to prepare the evening meal. There used to be an old Maire stump by the Ohutu Stream Hut and one log from it would keep burning all evening. You had to sharpen the axe a few times, though, for each hunk of wood that you hacked from it. Maire is tough wood. Later, when I got there, Jim had a great culler's fire going and the heat almost drove us all out from the oven-like heat reflected back from the mouthoid walls and roof.

Down into the creek and up the other side, I quickly found the first two deer that had fallen where they stood hit by the two, two four three bullets, one from a Sako Forester and the other from a BSA Majestic. My one was lying in a small gully twenty yards from where it had stood. I tailed them all and then started to track the fourth one in and out of the sloping clear spots, where the grass grew long and lush, and around the clumps of trees under girded with stinging nettles and Hookgrass.

I crept along following the path of freshly bent grasses where the hind had passed and the obvious route when there was no other sign in the dry summer conditions. Suddenly, WOOF, she barked and I spun in her direction to see her vanishing into the trees she had spotted me from. Continuing to creep on, now a little flustered by the fact that I had missed a chance through not seeing her, I poked my nose around the extended branches edging the open bits, as slowly and inconspicuously as possible, and suddenly, WOOF, she was gone again.

Four times that happened over the ten minutes that I pushed on on her trail. Those deer can be the most infuriating. They don't have the decency to run away in a manner that you know will take them out of reasonable reach in a few minutes. They just bark and fluff off a few yards to watch you approach again from a hidden position where they have all the advantages over you. When you think that they have really gone this time and relax your concentration a bit, they bark at you again, jolting your senses, and you see their tantalizing tail disappearing into the bushes yet again. Often you never get them.

But not this time. Out of nowhere she materialized about ten yards down the slope below in a clear spot, broad side on, watching me. She must have given up the game. The rifle in my hands shot to my shoulder and BOOM, she fell. But it wasn't me that had fired!

When she fell, I was able to see there on the other side of her was the other culler that had been with us. From back up on the track he had heard the hind barking at me as I had closed on her time after time, and had decided to come and give me a hand. His two four three bullet hadn't penetrated right through the deer, thank goodness, as I was directly in line. Mind you, he would have been directly in line with my shot too if I had been a little bit faster. But the point is, he shouldn't have been there at all.

It was a dangerous decision he made to come over the creek, knowing that I wouldn't know he was there. It caused a breach between us and I left the job a few days later because of it. I wished I hadn't now as it was a rash decision, but there it was. A few years meat hunting, possum trapping and rabbiting lay ahead for me.

It was twenty-eight years later that I next saw him and I enjoyed the chat that we had, and hope to do it some more. He is a good guy. A lot of people, including me, do some stupid things at times. It is a part of being human. But we can react in ways that we later regret and are sorry for. The ability to be gracious to ourselves and others is a great quality and the one the we need to be the most gracious to most often is ourselves.

There was one other stray that I came across. This one wasn't a bullet. It had its beginnings like this.

One night after I had been many days alone in the bush, when a man's beginning to forget what a human voice is like, and the sudden awareness of another's presence gives an inner alarm, I had an occurrence that was a mystery for several years before being resolved in a coincidental way. I was hunting in a wide, sweeping, and lost to many, valley of the northern Tararuas out of a simple hut, carrying out the deer that I shot to pay for the next lot of food that I would need to come back and hunt some more. Evening was making a long slow arrival after an overcast day and I headed down the little creek where the trickle that it managed was only evident where one narrow, deep silent pool emptied into another. The higher branches of the trees and the fronds of the exceptionally high pungas on each side reached out and often met speckling the moss-covered rocks that I drifted over with the pattern of the sky. It was, and is, a beautiful environment and I was greatly enjoying the solitude and quietness of a place that seldom sees man, so its wonder exists for itself or God's sake alone. I was heading for some clearings that I knew and that deer often came to feed in, in the days dying light.

I noticed an eel in the creek. It was not a particularly big or notable one. I was just surprised to see it there, for downstream I knew there to be a huge canyon-like waterfall preceded by a long gorge of many drops, all unable to be negotiated by an eel. Over the watershed in the other direction, which is a deep saddle, the river that flowed out the other side of the range had even bigger waterfalls of up to two hundred feet that an eel would find absolutely impossible to navigate too. So, to see this eel was amazing and I wondered how it had managed to get there.

Musing on that, I carried on, as I was intent on getting a deer to pay for an upcoming trip to Fiordland with the Deerstalkers Association to cull a few Wapiti. That trip was organized by John Anderson and I was recently thrilled to see a photo in his book 'The Eye of the Hunter" that was taken by John Muir from Feilding. I happened to be with him the day that he took that photo.

Anyway, on the return trip an hour later, when the shade of the creek was getting pretty deep, and without a deer, I again looked for the eel in the pool. It wasn't there. I quickly scouted around in the two adjacent pools just out of interest. I wasn't busy and could spare the moments, having no pressing appointments for a week or three. Nope, it wasn't there. Strange. I couldn't imagine where it had gone. The water was crystal clear and there were no overhanging edges for it to have hidden under. Then, as

At Home in the Hills

I swung on along the edge of the stream, splashing through the very still flat water as I crossed, I saw it. It was hanging in a slash made in a punga near the creek, dead!

Suddenly, the uneasy feeling exploded within me of there being someone near. After so long alone that feeling is very unnerving. The calmness and simple peace of heart and mind that solitude in the bush imparts had fled and was replaced with tenseness and a kind of uncertain alarm. I felt like crouching and slinking off into a hiding place. I must have been alone too long. I called out twice but no one answered my call. So I nervously continued on to the hut, constantly looking behind me as I went and expecting that I would either have company at the hut when I arrived, or at least before the night was set in. Not many people knew about that hut so the options were limited. However there was no one there and through the night no one arrived.

There were no other huts in the valley at that time and there would have been no time for a person to walk out of the valley before dark. Whoever had killed that eel was sleeping somewhere near, and it was a strange night that I spent wondering who, what and where.

On traveling out a few days later, the farmer at the end of the road told me he had not seen any cars on the road and had not given permission for anyone to cross his property, which was the only realistic access to that valley. Weeks passed, years passed, and the mystery just remained. I adjusted myself to thinking that I would never know who had been there and why they hadn't come to the hut.

This was about nineteen sixty-eight. I've got the kind of memory that never seems to lose details or forget incidents, so the picture of that eel hanging in the punga haunted me for a long time. I can still see it there now, thirty years later.

After Denise and I married in nineteen seventy-one and I

realized that the lifestyle of the hills that I had lived would not be possible anymore, I began to work for the Manawatu Pest Destruction Board. In ordinary language it was the Rabbit Board. I suppose rabbiters are called Noxious Animal Life Termination Technicians now, or some such politically correct title. Anyway, my block was the Shannon one and consisted of ninety thousand acres of farmland between the Manawatu River and the bush edge at the top of the Tararua foothills, ranging from just south of Shannon almost to Linton.

The hunting that we did then as rabbiters was with dogs and shotguns, starting at dawn, whenever that happened to be, for the following eight hours. Some of the guys on the other blocks were real characters coming from many walks of life, and a book could be written about them alone. It was a good job for me at the time, and I loved working with the variety of dogs of all shapes and sizes that became my friends through the long days that we roamed together.

We categorized all the conglomeration of color, size and shape simply in two types, running dogs and sniffing dogs. I particularly liked to watch the greyhound and whippet types running down a rabbit or hare in an open paddock after it had been sniffed out of cover by one of the sniffing dogs. Their speed and the action of their running were a sight that I marveled at. A few were killed by trains and stray shotgun pellets, not from my shotgun, which broke my heart on occasions. I love dogs and the companionship that they can give.

One day I was working the bush edge at the top of the hills east of the Manawatu plains and came across a very interesting character. Henry Irwin was his name and he had grown up at Opiki on the family dairy farm but had slowly transferred his home to a hut on a plateau on the bush edge just south of the Tokomaru River. I remember that he told me of the opossums that he had befriended and would come to be fed at his door each evening, and many other things. Many, many other things. In fact it took me four hours to get away from him after I had said my first goodbye. He talked so much. I guess that he didn't have many people to talk to from day to day. I don't know what Henry did with his time, but I guessed that with all the elbowroom of the Ranges behind his place, he would have roamed wide and far over the years that he had been there.

I don't remember much of what we talked about but one thing that came up in conversation I think I will never forget. From where I met him some distance from his hut on a windswept ridge covered in poor quality grazing, we could see back into the Tararuas with a wide sweeping view. I casually said to him, as we squinted off into the distance, that I had hunted extensively up in that valley that could be almost seen in the far off haze. He said, "Yeah, I went up there once some years ago. I got an eel in the creek.".......There was a long pregnant pause as my mind did a regurgitation and came up with the old mystery. "And you made a slash in a punga and hung it there didn't you?" I asked in return. "Yeah!" he said in amazement.

We had almost met some years before and he was the person who had given me that uneasy night. I thought how it would have been a pleasant evening if we had met that time, although after second thoughts I wondered if I would have been able to get any sleep if he had been as verbose then as he was at this time. He was surprised that there had been someone so close and he hadn't known it at all at the time. He also hadn't known that there was a hut up there.

I saw Henry again only once more and that was on the next year's circuit of the hilltops for the Pest Destruction Board. I saw him at a distance; he saw me at the same time and sloped off into the bush, hiding from the indiscernible bloke he could see approaching. However I persevered and found him, and we had a cup of tea out of very doubtful mugs. He was more reclusive that time and the visit was not nearly as long as the first.

So the mystery was solved. Amazing how these things can happen. It's a great place the bush and the mountains. Those that populate it are a unique many faceted breed. It's different these days though. It used to be that only the very keen types got back more than a days walk from the farms and so anyone that you met back there was similar to yourself and good company at anyone's fire. The cowboys and beer can hunters were only found on the bush edge camps. Now with the high usage of helicopters you can find anyone anywhere.

The types that I find the hardest to stomach in the bush are the egotists. They stand with their feet about three feet apart, arms folded high on their chests, and speak loudly, as if you're either deaf or in the distance, spouting off eloquently about the dozens of deer they have shot. They apparently know all the ballistics about all the calibres and have views so unbending and strong about what are the best ones for deer at what ranges, etcetera, that you feel that if you don't yell back rather than talk at a normal level you're just not the man that they are.

I had one guy ridicule me, loud enough for others a hundred yards away to hear, for only owning two rifles. I have a deer rifle and a twenty two. When I asked him how many rifles he has he answered, twenty-six. He said you need some for bush hunting, some for longer distance, some for rabbits, goats and goodness knows what else. He would need several gun bearers each time that he goes hunting and the noise that they would make would frighten any deer nearby into the next range. I hope he keeps away from any huts that I end up in for the night.

You learn a lot as the years go along, mostly about yourself. The bush changes you. The challenges and trials expand your self-awareness and even the cowboys and beer can boys can put a something into your character.

Henry was a character. I saw his photo in a book many years later. It was that book that had photos from all over New Zealand in it all taken in a single day, I think. Henry used to go down to the Tokomaru dump each day, a walk of some miles, to get newspapers. The photo was taken at the dump early in the morning and there was his smiling face again. I wonder if you're still there Henry. One of the rooms of his hut was full of old newspapers. I guess that was the way that he kept his mind occupied and learnt of the happenings of the world.

This says a bit about the kind of thing that causes changes in you as you battle your way through a life addicted to the bush and the love of wilderness, better, perhaps, than other ways.

BUSH GROWTH

I crossed the watershed from the Punga Hut, late one afternoon.
I crossed this maze of little ridges and tiny streams.
There's a faint old trail blazed there, 'neath ferns and 'tween the trees,
It's a jungle of a million shadows in browns and greens.

Then up the Toko stream I slip through slow and silent pools,
That trouble briefly as warmly greeting, I pass by.
And into the rocky cool of a kiekie cluttered gorge,
Boots leap nimbly as I glimpse the dimming sky.

Quickly scale the waterfall into this remnant rivers head,
Up the slip to a secret gap in the leatherwood wall.
I slow up near the ridge top, near a clearing that I knew
For if I'm puffing I can't be sure the deer will fall.

Stray Bullets, Stray People

Then there, upon the ridge, a spiker sharp against the sky,
  Silhouetted in the sunset of a summer day.
A hundred yards, two hundred, in that light I couldn't tell,
  So fired carefully, he leaped and rushed away.

Found him lying in the clearing and as the light was fading out
  Dressed him quickly and moved off fast to get back home.
The bush grew dark as I raced through and that watershed yet to cross,
  I found a friendly star to guide me through the gloom.

The lights went out, there was no moon, I was blind but for my star
  Which played hide and seek midst the leaves way overhead.
  With my arm before my eyes and rifle held in front
  I edged my way back onto the cold damp watershed.

All so silent on I went, slowly cautiously placed each foot.
  Climbed over, under and through things I couldn't see.
I followed that star for hours wondering where I'd sleep that night,
  In my hut or amongst the leaves beside a tree.

Then quite nearby I heard the trickle of a slightly larger stream
  So walked right in and felt the current with my hand.
It goes my way, it may be the one that passes by the hut,
  I followed the water, the slimy rocks, the silt and sand.

Finally, back in the hut, fire blazing, billies slung,
  No one missed me, no one worried, I was alone.
A soul building day I think better than the tinsel of the towns.
  I was taller, have townies ever grown?

Chapter Seven
Lonely Times

∽

I don't know if it's the same for everyone, but I have had some very lonely times and weird subsequent experiences during times alone in the hills. I guess I would say that I have been a lonely person, particularly as a teenager. I think loneliness is a part of being human, to some degree, at least in this life.

In my family I have a brother and sister, both older than I, and neither of them is like me or fully enjoys doing the same things that I do. The nearest friends that I could be with when younger lived some miles away, and, although I walked the miles along country roads to their place at weekends, I had a lot of time to fill in alone. I guess that this was the start of my enjoying the outdoors alone. I was on my own when I shot my first deer, most of the tramping and hunting that I have done and most of the deer that I have shot throughout my life till today have been shot without company. I have always said that one person makes too much noise when hunting and so two make much too much noise, however it's nice to have good company at the hut or campsite in the evenings. It has not always been available to me.

When I was in my late teens I had several strange experiences that disturbed me a lot at the time. I didn't know then that if you deprive yourself psychologically of needed input then your brain would manufacture that input for you artificially. It's a natural phenomenon, but on the times that I experienced this thing I didn't know that, and so had not a little disquiet from it. Let me explain.

One time my brother and I had dropped off the ridge between what was then called West Peak and the knob called Dennen in the Tararuas. It was lousy weather and we had hoped to be able to do the loop walk around the main Range including Feild, Vosseler, Maungahuka, Anderson Memorial and Waitewaiwai huts returning to the Otaki forks where we left our car.

However, the weather forbade it, so after reaching Vosseler Hut in what is often meaninglessly termed "inclement weather" in hut logs books around the hills, we decided to head for the Waiotauru River for a bit of hunting instead. No one ever uses the word inclement except in log books in the hills, as far as I can gather, so I guess it's an effort by those of us who have had little education to sound educated. When you think about it maybe it works.

Backtracking over West Peak, we headed down towards Feild Hut trying to guess where Dennen was in the roaring pea soup that blasted out of the Waiotauru River below us, so we could drop off into the soup bowl after passing Dennen rather before it. However, we dropped off too soon in the cloud and ended up clambering down into the headwaters of Tregear Creek. It was lowering yourself carefully through the tussock and leatherjacket, holding on with everything you had available sort of stuff. Even eyebrows and tongues can be useful when you're desperate on a steep climb like that, or so I hear.

After reaching the comparative level of the creek proper, we began traipsing off down the creek expecting to find a campsite before dark and build a bivouac out of ferns etc. We surprised two stags on slips in almost identical places, and, with the amount of deer sign there decided that this was a place for later greater

Lonely Times

examination. We camped out as planned in the lower reaches of Tregear creek, and a clear and enjoyable evening and night followed for us under ferns leaned against a branch.

My brother never did go back there. However a few weeks later I returned alone, and intending to go back up the same creek, made a wrong turn and ended up in Snowy Creek. Here I discovered the tent camp that used to be there, quite accidentally. It was pretty typical of the type, having, as I remember, two sack slung bunks one much wider than the other. I decided to have a look at this creek, seeing that I had no time to backtrack and go up the other stream that I had originally intended to explore.

While walking up that creek there in the evening, a most unusual sound filled my ears. I was wading upstream thigh deep through a small gorge and came up to a flow of rapids that rushed over a wide flat before plunging into the darkness and cold where I was. Knowing that over the rocks and around the bend there was a large grassy flat, I battled my way across the current preparing to sneak out onto the flat, eyes alert for any deer that may be there.

Suddenly, a strange sound, alien to my surroundings, invaded the gorge all around me, emanating from the clearing around the bend. In a way that seemed to be completely natural, I could hear a country school picnic in full swing on the flat ahead. There were the sounds of the fathers calling to their children to run faster. I could hear the mothers having a sack race. There were whistles and a loud speaker telling people where to get their hotdogs. I could hear the voices of children yelling and laughing, etc, etc, etc. The coconut shy, the lolly scramble, the shooting gallery, all were there as their sounds filled my ears. It was all so real and natural sounding to me, and I never realized how ludicrous and out of place a school picnic would be there.

I ran up through the rapids and around onto the flat, motivated by a sudden, acute feeling of loneliness that had been with me in a smaller way the whole of the last few days. I couldn't see them! They must be in the trees at the end of the flat, I thought, so I ran over into the trees. No one was there! Where were they? Then it all cleared and the reality of where I was and the stupidity of what I had been thinking and doing descended on me. It was all in my mind. No one was there. I remember sitting down on a fallen tree and crying and crying - not because of the people that weren't there, but because of the terrible pain of loneliness that gripped my guts. Funny experience, and at the time I had no explanation for it. It was a long time before I told anyone about it either.

Another time when I was culling, I was traveling the lower part of the Pourangaki River one evening on a perfect day. Deer had been few in the week that I had been hunting the sides of that magnificent valley that soared up to wide tussock slopes above the bush line and ended on the variety of peak shapes majestically established there. I had been lonely but to no great degree, particularly.

A few days earlier I had been climbing over a log jam when some of the logs that I was standing on suddenly gave way, and I crashed to the ground landing heavily on my back. I was unhurt, probably due to the fitness that I had, but my rifle didn't do so well. A four inch diameter log, about ten feet in length, landed end on on my rifle scope and had broken the mounts.

It was impossible to do anything about it and I was disappointed. At least I had a steel barreled scope sight and it had not been damaged, except to distort the front with a big dent, so that it wasn't round anymore. The waterproofing and adjustments for zeroing still worked perfectly. I had an even more spectacular fall in Fiordland two years later that dented the other side of the front on the same scope, yet again it still worked faultlessly. A good steel tubed scope is a real asset if you are spending a lot of time in the bush because those accidents will happen sometime. Fitness is your best personal protection.

Anyway, rounding the extremity of a huge log rammed into the river on a bend, on one of many in the lower reaches of the river, and again wading in water up to my thighs, I suddenly heard the sound of babies crying. There were two of them somewhere near. I glanced, as anyone would, fully expecting to see them probably with an adult seated on a rock against the bank, where the river flow in flood found its limits. No one was there of course. The sound and feeling passed in a brief moment, that time, but still left me with the sharp feeling of loneliness again. Those were the only times that that sort of thing happened to me but it was an example of a phenomenon associated with loneliness. I hope that I never experience it again.

Loneliness is a funny thing. It's painful too. Hellishly so. To me it's the greatest pain that I have ever known. It differs from aloneness. You can be alone and yet not lonely. Also you can be lonely and yet not alone. People in the city, I think, can be the loneliest people in the world. But when you are alone and there are not the sounds of people around for long periods of time and loneliness arrives, your mind can make up the sounds and illusions that your psyche needs.

I can't imagine why I should have needed a school picnic at that time in the Waiotauru River, but that is what my mind cooked up. I don't have a particular affinity for babies either, so I don't know why that was the thing that I heard. The wonders of the mind, I suppose. You may be beginning to think that I am nuts and wondering why you are reading this. Well, I think that this sort of thing is not uncommon to people that have spent a lot of time alone. Maybe not many people talk about it. But those experiences, and others that differ, have happened to me, and have caused me to realize that there are many different motivations in the souls of those of us who love the hills, and not all of them are we conscious of.

What is it that makes us hunters and mountain lovers the way we are? I am sure that it is predominantly an enjoyment of nature that is in all people but perhaps a little stronger in us. However, the people that enjoy the hills also enjoy physical exertion to a large degree. A greater level of love of silence may be born into us, the most beautiful music there is in the right environment. We are also people that are able to entertain ourselves in our own thoughts to a large degree. A man once asked me what I think about when I am away in the hills alone for days at a time. Everything on earth imaginable I replied.

But also, and in some parts of many of us, I am sure that it is fair to say, there is not only the drawing of the hills and the wide open spaces and the things that we can exercise deep in our natures but there can also be a pushing from behind. I mean there can be things from our lives in society that we want to get away from. These push us to find refuge in a safe place away from society. We can have had hurtful experiences with people that find a balm in the solitude of the mountains. We can have unresolved worries that we find relief and escape from in the hills.

For some, the hills can be a refuge from inner turmoil. The turmoil remains but there is relief in the wonders of the wild. These things can push us into the hills at the same time as we can be drawn by our love of the wilderness. It can be a part of the whole for some of us.

I wrote the poems below about this enigma within me. A full life consists of a fullness of emotions. The life without contemplation is not worth living said Socrates. A life that is lived on the surface only and denies the deep feelings of our humanity is a farce in my book. "Know thyself" said Plato. The hills surely teach you a lot about yourself. The Bible, too, tells us that for everything there is a season. A time for tears, and a time for laughter. These poems are about some times for tears that have occurred in my life on the hill.

The first one is about a time when I was meat hunting. The days of hunting were interspersed with trips to town to sell the animals I carried out, with brief visits to my parents' home and short times spent with friends. Then I would face the road to the bush again, and days of the routine of sleep, fire lighting and cooking, hours of endless bush walking, moments of action as a deer was sighted and shot, hours of puffing under the weight of a heavy deer carcass, then sleep and so the cycle continued. It could be wonderful, and usually was, but there were moments of another kind.

JUST ANOTHER DEER

In the distant dense bush of Miro Valley
Against the wall of the hut I sat
At the end of a showery day.
Up on Bull Knob a deer in the lee
Of the ridge so with rifle and hat
Strolled round the hut and away.

Thunder announced, drenched I will be
But wove steadily along the deer trails
To the deer that was already dead.
Yet he blissfully fed browsing quietly
In the stillness before storm does prevail.
Dead his carcass was heavy as lead.

Forked lightening flickered constantly,
Thunder rolled on and on deafeningly,
Crashing raindrops advanced on me steadily,

At Home in the Hills

Mind excited by stillness and activity
And the might of the flashing electricity,
But bored inside, blank, dull and lonely.

Drenched to the skin with rain and blood,
Another deer dead, another shot fired.
A few more dollars to buy petrol and food,
A lonely life but of all else I'd tired.
Yet hunting was great when I was in the mood.
Blue tonight, lonely tea, lonely hut, lonely fire

This next poem is based on a hunter that I observed one time, and, although I don't know if it is a true representation of his particular inner state, it's how he struck me. I know that it can be true of many of us, at least to some extent. It certainly is true of myself in some ways.

STORM IN A STORM

Rivers roaring through the leaves,
Branches waving wild.
Curling clouds, the skies do grieve,
Wind lashed mountain side.
Tussock flashing, whipping back,
Punishing the peaks.
On the raging ridge in mountain gear
Defiant stands the weak.

Hardy brow and weathered cheek
Both crowding out his eyes.
The gale it seems does from him speak,
He embodies the winds weird cries.

Lonely Times

*Inside the shell a broken heart
That home and friend had left.
Pain drove him to a life apart,
To bed in mountain cleft.*

*An expert now in highland lore,
Can teach not what he knows.
Despises those he's known before
Who live in concrete rows.
Yet all he knows is how to live
And love to live as free,
From all the human bondages
To comfort and luxury.*

*Strong of limb the slopes did train
His heart and lungs to strength.
Yet weak and weaker he does wane,
His soul will die at length.
Oh saddest man, how proud you are
Though home within the storm,
A storm prevails
within your heart,
Lost, wounded, alone, forlorn.*

This next poem is written of my state of mind during the day in the Pourangaki when I heard the babies crying.

LONELINESS IN THE POURANGAKI

*It was lonely where I walked on the peaks last eve'
It's lonely again in the valleys today.
A weeks passed all alone in this tangle of trees,*

At Home in the Hills

The only sound is where trickling streams play.
All is so still, the sky boring blue
Like a picture some young artist drew.

And I climb 'round the canvas, nothing lives here,
No one would hear even my rifles great shout.
I live in these hills and I'm paid to shoot deer
But where they've gone I cannot work out.
Bored and alone in this lost mountain canyon,
Lonely thoughts make a dismal companion.

Then a deer on that spur, but I've missed, fire again,
The second shot clean misses too.
He's gone. Was he there? Despair, lonely pain,
I think of home. Should I go some place new?
Will things ever look up? Will the weather ever change?
Will I ever find deer on this mountain range.

And this last poem is about the other side of the coin, just to balance the picture properly. Its interesting that good weather doesn't necessarily make a wonderful time, and bad weather makes a bad time.

R*AIN*

The chill of the water soaks down my boots,
It's freezing but I really don't mind.
This is my world, here I've planted my roots,
Yes, discomfort but beauty abounds.
These mountains treasures I've joyfully mined,
Upstream now a waterfall sounds.

Lonely Times

Rain pounding my parka and soaked to the skin,
Face turned from the blistering gusts.
But fresh air is free through the hills that I'm in
And I'm young and I'm fit and I'm free.
Squelching upstream, my heart fairly busts,
There's nowhere that I'd rather be.

The river is rising, I'll cross it no more.
It's moving the boulders below.
A brown torrent of death, a deafening roar,
An awe filled wonderful day.
Out of the creek where the misty winds blow
On the ridge I go on my way.

Swinging along on the face of the ranges
In drenched bush and gale driven cloud.
Four or five hours I'll be out of the dangers
In the hut on the yet distant creek.
Now will be over but memories shroud
Will descend, and later lovingly speak.

It's interesting isn't it that both painful loneliness and wonderful solitude and aloneness can be present in the same person. They may be present in you too. One pulls you into the hills and the other pushes you in. You can't divide the two parts of us that push and pull us into the hills. We are too complex for that and life is just simply not that easy to define. But no matter, I think. In fact, what a blessing to us all that this is so. Because life is indefinable and beyond our mind's ability to fully comprehend it, it has the power to produce both wonder and awe. If we could fully understand ourselves and all that life is, we would soon be irrevocably and crushingly bored. A great cloud of deadness and hopelessness would descend over the entire human race, never to lift, so causing us all to live trapped in some horror that only a science fiction writer could devise. It is the unknown and unknowables of life that causes us to stand back with watery eyes and heart bursting joy and simply gaze upon a thing, finding fulfillment in the sight.

Understanding and analyzed, definitive knowledge can rob us of the enjoyment of that kind of thing. It is because of the existence of that which we don't comprehend that we are able to really enjoy life. The known always has the tendency to become boring in the end. The unknown always retains its fascination. That's why the next bend in a river and the distant ridge draw our hearts, whose dreams compel our feet to go that little bit further before resting, or bring us back to the hills after a particularly harrowing trip.

A very wild red haired Dutchman shouted out across a building site that I worked on for a few weeks once, words that I have never forgotten." If you don't learn something every day you may as well cut your throat". There were times that I am sure that he hadn't taken his own advice to learn something every day, as his learning seemed definitely limited in some social graces. However, he had a point, and learning is the exploration of the unknown. To learn is to live, I think, and to live is to learn. Life without the unknown would be intolerable, and the greatest unknown is ourselves.

Strive as we will to understand ourselves, we will never fully do it, and that is the greatest comfort and the greatest frustration. It is not comfortable to lack understanding of yourself, but imagine the horror of knowing yourself absolutely in all ways. No surprises left. All reactions known and regulated. All thoughts and ideals set in concrete. Nothing to develop within, all done.

BOREDOM COMPLETE

It is comforting to know that that will never happen. We need to accept and to learn to treasure the unknowableness of ourselves. We need to learn to enter into full appreciation of that which is beyond our understanding and simply gaze at the wonder. That is what watching a sunset is all about. It's what gazing into a fire is all about. It is what watching a full blown, mature, rutting stag in the wild is all about. It's what mountains are all about and it's what the joy of life in the wilderness springs from.

It is the unknown in ourselves that makes life spicy and interesting, even fascinating, even inspiring. So the things that cause us to like and enjoy the bush and the hills, complex as they may be and probably not understandable, are the things that in the long run make it so wonderful for us.

I often think of the question asked of mountaineers who risk all to reach the top of a mountain, and even the guy who crossed Antarctica recently, "Why do you do it?" There is no answer to that. If a person has to ask that question it reveals, irreversibly, that they would not understand the answer if it was able to be articulated and given to them.

Joy, wonder, laughter, tears, pain, struggle, health, excess fitness, exhilaration, loneliness, silence, sadness, wonderful solitude, reflection of self, and in fact every valid human emotion, and some not so valid. All are part of life in the hills and life spent alone. Every one of them adds to the wonder of it all.

Chapter Eight
The Odd Few Deer

Sleeping Stag

It was a hot summer day and the air was still over the whole valley that I was hunting in. The main creek in the centre of the valley was running low. The full power of summer had denied it an ample complement to its crystalline life that quietly bubbled and gurgled its way through the overhanging pungas, amidst the shadows of the towering giants blocking the sky from my view. Moss, covering the rocks on and around the edges of the creek that I was making my way along, in the cool of that place, made my footfalls soft and inaudible. The Sako 243 slung in my right hand felt good. My hand rocked it back and forward from time to time so that the half closed bolt would hit against the back of my right wrist, reassuring me that I hadn't inadvertently knocked it closed, thereby fully cocking it and setting myself up for possible tragedy. It was a habit that I had acquired while culling some years before and had become automatic. I was a tuned hunter in a well known environment, young and fit and free.

Something, almost imperceptible, about the way the bush shadowed ridge on my right breathed in the sun drenched valley, drew me away from the creek, and I began to slowly creep

At Home in the Hills

through the tangle of scrub up the slope to the ridge proper where I knew it would be more open. Bending and twisting in, around, under and over every branch and frond so as to minimize noise, time not an issue, I hunted my way along with strength and fitness to burn, enjoying every moment of this wonderful day. The bush seemed to be embracing me and I felt fully at peace. My eyes probed every nuance of shadow variation, and, pausing continuously, I examined the secrets of this patch of bush, identifying everything before classifying it, rejecting it as not what I was seeking, and sweeping on to new realms.

I was occasionally glancing at the ground in front and unconsciously memorizing the next three or four steps. My feet, surrounded in lace up gumboots enhanced by the addition of heel plates held on with horseshoe nails whose heads protruded giving excellent grip on rocks, rotting and slippery logs, steep grassy slopes and clay slips etc., cautiously shifted weight from one to the other. I felt the dry leaves and twigs crush into the damp earth of the forest floor, sometimes rocking back as a twig felt underfoot warned any more pressure would cause it to crack and make the dreaded happen. Noise.

The grey Swanndri bush shirt that I was wearing made passage through the crown fern clumps that I passed here and there as silent as possible. My bare legs, browned by the weather and scratched by endless scrub, leatherjacket and hidden bushlawyer, protruded from black rugby shorts which kept me cool and comfortable on this hot day in slow but continuous movement. I was reveling in it all.

Suddenly, a single sound. I became a motionless; all of my senses reached high alert in an instant. What was that? I guess like a computer every known sound that I'd ever heard in the bush raced through my mind trying to make a match. Zero. Then what could it have been? There's only one sound it could have been. It had to be the sound of an antler softly bumping against a small tree trunk. Where did it come from? I waited. A few minutes later, there it was again. About fifty yards ahead, slightly to the right of my travel path I reckoned. So how do I move from here? Slowly and keeping the thickest scrub and biggest trees in front of me.

Much slower now I made my way from cover to cover, peering through the leaves of each bush where possible rather than looking over or around to avoid silhouetting myself. Ten yards and no sound from me or the nearby stag. Twenty. Thirty. I was coming through a heavily scrubbed piece so carefully even the leaves didn't know that I was there, I think. The ground up front was clearer, and around a large trunk five yards further on was a large area devoid of undergrowth. He'll be here, if I can just make it to that tree trunk, I thought.

A minute later my face slowly edged around the tree. Twenty feet in front of me, with his feet tucked up under him and with his sleepy eyes closed on his sun spotted droopy head barely supported at half-mast between two small tree trunks, lay the stag. In his drowsy state he had bumped his antlers on the nearby tree trunks as he had been trying to resist lowering his head to the ground in full slumber, much the same way that a tired driver's head can fall and then suddenly jerk up again.

He never knew how he died. His sleep just deepened. As I walked over to him with the rifle shot echoing back from the distant ridge behind me, his legs were still tucked up under him and his eyes were closed. His head had finally rested between the small trees and his struggle to keep awake was over. My immediate financial problems were over too. But now the work would begin. It was a four-hour walk out to my car and between there and where this stag lay was a hill big enough to exact a lot of sweat, especially on a day like this one.

At Home in the Hills

A top culler had once said lightheartedly that you're not a real hunter until you can shoot deer in their sleep. It was nice to reflect at that time that the first deer that I ever shot was asleep. The first deer that I shot on my first day as a contract hunter for the Forestry was also a sleeping stag and the second a sleeping hind. This one was asleep too. It's fun to get so close.

Tiny Hind

It was a blustery, windy day and Ross and I made our way through the pepperwood and flax that clogged a small creek that was getting ever smaller. It was cold. We had our swanndris done up tight to our necks, and our bare legs were goosebumpy as the gusts of cold air blasted us when we hit clear spots above old fallen logs that leaned against the stream side and were covered in bushlawyer and unmentionably impassable gunge.

From time to time we came across grassy spots on the creek where the stream trickled over small brown stones that seemed more the color of clay than rock. It was pretty. The sides of the stream on both sides held mostly stunted trees, which whooshed and whistled at us as the wind slashed at their tops. Occasional leatherjacket clumps intruded down to the creek bed and gave warning that the going in the creek was going to become more difficult, and perhaps impossible. It was a dirty, uncomfortable, inhospitable and wonderful place to be.

Ross' green swanndri leaped out of sight off a log spanning the creek, propelled by his lace up gumboots twenty yards in front of me. As I topped the log, I was just in time to see his right shoulder, suspending the typical crooked arm of a hunter grasping his rifle - a BSA Majestic 308 - disappear around a huge boulder as the creek took a turn to the left and into new vistas. As I made the boulder and followed, leaping across the water of the creek for perhaps the thousandth time that day, I noticed

The Odd Few Deer

Ross still about twenty yards in front, eyes intent on the difficult creek bed he was negotiating there. I paused for breath and a look around. The creek and sides were clearer here. Still, there was much scrubby rubbish, which is the name that I have given to bushes that I don't know the names of, but do know the difficulty of pushing through. But the scrubby rubbish was now separated with clumps of toi toi, flax, open rock, and areas of short grasses of differing types. The wind was howling through it all. Ross didn't seem to feel conditions that I would shrink from, and he seldom seemed to tire either. This was not nearly bad enough for him to hear any suggestion that we should head out of here for more comfortable places. There was fresh deer sign all the way up the dirty little creek and we really needed one.

Suddenly there was a hind running up the left side of the creek through a clearing about fifty feet above me and about forty yards away. How had I missed her? Where had she come from? There was nowhere that she could have been hiding. But there she was, a testimony to either the ethereal substance of a hunted animal, or the malady of the sudden and unexplainable blindness that can strike the hunter. I was soon to find out that there was another reason.

She was running directly away from me, and Ross, completely oblivious to her, turned casually around to check on my progress. He saw my rifle flashing to my shoulder with the bolt being depressed to full cock on the way. The bounding hind was more side on to him and he was able to see it clearly panicked at full flight up hill and angling away. The post of my Pecar scope hit the white spot of the departing deer and I fired. She dropped. All over in a second or two.

A wry smile passed between Ross and I as we flicked our eyebrows up and down briefly to each other, uniting us again across the physical and mental solitude the terrain and weather had formed between us. I made my way over some old slippery logs and, grabbing a few handfuls of ground fern, hauled my way up over the flood line bank onto the level above where the slope of the hillside began. Slanting up through the tall grass and dodging my way around the scrubby bushes, I made my way up to where the deer had been when I fired. All thought of the wind and cold had been eclipsed by the appearance of the deer, the light rush of adrenaline and the feelings that a successful hunt brings. Casting my eyes here and there I moved confidently along knowing that the deer was dead. It had nowhere to go on this clearish slope and so I knew that it was laying just here, about where I was looking. But where was the darn thing? I must have gone past it.

Back and forward I went over ground that couldn't hide the hide of this obviously mature hind. After a minute or two in which Ross had settled down for one of his smokes, I still couldn't find it. Ross looked at me quizzically and I could read his thoughts. What are you mucking around at? It has to be just where you are standing. But it wasn't. There was only that long, broad leafed grass all around the spot, except for a small bush about two feet high and two feet round. It just wasn't there. But it had to be. I wandered about some more and yelled to Ross to confirm if I was at the right spot. Yes, it had to be right where I was standing.

Then, under the tiny bush that I hadn't taken a second look at, I spotted the familiar color of deerskin. I saw a foot. A tiny foot. Grabbing it I pulled the deer out and raised it above my head with one hand. It was the tiniest deer that I had ever seen. A fully mature hind with aged eyeteeth in her upper jaw but only the size of a month old fawn. It had the coloring of an adult deer, and even the coarse texture of an adult red deer's hide. There was nothing on it edible, even the skin was totally ruined by the passage of the one hundred and ten grain bullet through its length. From a tough, go where no one else goes, brave the elements hunter, and successful hero of the fast running shot in the vast fastnesses of the wild, I passed to a wimpish murderer and mutilator of tiny, toy deer. It embarrassed me to have found and shot such a animal. We left it there hidden under a bush where, hopefully, no one else would ever find it - ashamed of ourselves - and continued on never to mention it again, but had no luck the rest of the day.

Looking back later, I realized at least two redeeming features of that incident. Firstly, because the deer was so small it made the running shot so much the better, and one that I should be proud of. I don't feel that though, even today. There are some shots that I feel proud of, and most of the best ones were pulled off when I was alone, but that one doesn't feature in the "proud of myself" gallery of my private mind.

Secondly, how lucky we were to have come across such an animal. Whether it was a dwarf deer or simply undernourished I don't know. I do remember that we commented on how perfectly proportioned it was at the time, so I don't think that it would be a result of malnutrition. Very strange. I wish I had been in the habit of taking a camera with me in those days. I still forget to do that more often than not, even now.

THE CHASE

It was on a spring day I found myself edging my way higher and higher up a ridge that slanted northwards, reaching for the sullen gray of an overcast evening sky that hung heavily over the Maropea River. Chris Satherley and I, both working for the New Zealand Forestry Service in the paradise of the Northwest Ruahines block at the time, had waded and boulder-hopped our way up the rocky and shady Maropea river from the newly built Otukota Hut perched on a hidden terrace above the gorgy forks of the Waikamaka river. The days that we had spent hunting around the Otukota area had proven to be of mixed success and we were heading on to try our luck on new ground.

The hut at Maropea forks has been renovated now, and as yet I haven't seen it, but that spot is as good a spot to be when the sun shines as a hunter could possibly wish for. It's not too bad when a Ruahine storm thunders up the valley either, as I experienced one time a year or two later.

The night and day of that storm are etched on my memory well when the wind could be heard coming long before it hit the forks, blasting up the valley, roaring like a runaway train, lashing the trees, bending them over, hissing like a thousand steam engines through their upper branches, and booting the walls of the hut from all sides as it passed on and away to the upper valley that was bracing itself for this next onslaught.

Time and time again the wind howled reaching new levels of pain as it shrieked its way over my friend and I huddled in the recesses of the hut, trying to take it all in our stride. Rain poured heavily over those two days, and to fill the two gallon water container all it took was to hang it out the window for a minute or two and catch what fell off just two gutters of the corrugated iron roof. But all that was at another time and I'm getting sidetracked.

Arriving at the forks in the late afternoon with some short hours of daylight left, Chris decided to head up the creek from the hut to some clearings that he knew were only twenty minutes away, so I opted for the ridge to the north. The beech forest has long been my favorite to hunt in - the beautiful ground cover of dead beech leaves in all their variations of autumn colors, ranging through yellows and light tans to reds and deep browns. These tiny leaves sprinkle all over the dark earth and brilliant, almost iridescent green mosses cling to every rock, quietly rotting log, and mound pushed up by the unseen roots of massive beech trees standing so confidently and at peace on the tumbling hillsides.

Each tree grows so in harmony with the others around them. They do not encroach on the others' space, but, as they slowly over the years push themselves skyward together reaching for the life giving light, the quiet jostling of their outer extremities gently nudges for space, and room is taken and conceded in perfect unison. The leaves of each tree "fit" against all the others that they come in contact with at all levels, and the beauty is the kind that can only be truly honored by silence and the respect of moving through leaving no mark of passage.

It is this bush that I was hunting through as the day's end approached. My leather boots that were wearing holes in the toes and always wet from endless river travel, bound by strips of canvas as puttees, moved from silent moss to tree root to soft earth, one after another on and on and cautiously on up the ridge. I was clad in my black rugby shorts and a threadbare and torn checked woolen shirt of several browns held tight at the waist by my knife belt, weathered and shaped by years of hard use, also supporting a light green canvas Forestry issue culler's first aid kit.

Hanging from my curved right arm was the familiar weight of my BSA triple two topped by the four power Pecar scope zeroed perfectly. I looked and was the part. We needed meat for camp. I also needed tails for my monthly quota, which was not shaping up as I wanted it to.

Suddenly the sharp snap of a breaking twig cracked the air and bounced back to me from the ceiling of the giant beeches. Three leaping paces took me to the edge of the ridge, where the hill sloped away to the east down through the trunks of hundreds of trees. Thirty yards away a yearling hind was racing across the slope over the moss-covered logs and through the sparse undergrowth. I yelled out, "HEYYYY". She stopped out of sheer curiosity behind a huge tree some fifty yards off, at the edge of a steeper drop where she would have been out of sight. I waited, watching through my four-power scope, forefinger light on the trigger of the now fully loaded rifle.

Inevitably the face appeared looking directly at me over a small spindly twig of a tree beside the trunk that hid the rest of her. Fifty yards without a rest for my rifle at a small deer head in its smallest profile. I fired and she disappeared. Quickly moving down to the hill, I rounded the tree to find some spots of blood but no deer. Glancing around there she was about twenty yards away walking uphill away from me. A quick shot at the only target available dropped her with a broken back leg, and I walked up to her, leaned my rifle against a tree, and reached for my knife. That's where this hunt became totally different to any other.

When I was half way between the deer and where I had leaned my rifle - a distance of about ten feet she leapt to her three feet and ran.... downhill.....fast. In four seconds she would be out of sight. It would take three seconds to reach my rifle and she would be gone before I could fire. She could go a long way, and for a long time, on three legs motivated by the adrenaline that was now in her system. The day was nearly at an end and I may not find her tomorrow. We needed the meat and I wanted the tail. Only one option. I chased her as fast as I could go, fumbling to get the knife back into my sheath again.

It was all on. Both of us, over logs, through clumps of fern, down angling deer trails, leaping, slipping, falling over, rolling and racing on again, the yards flew out behind us and gathered in heaps up the forested hillside that I had not taken a good look at. We were both puffing hard and I had been closing on her. Now, only five or so yards and she, looking back with wide white eyes was near the end of her stamina. So was I.

A huge fallen log lay angling down the hill and, on the right hand side of it, that we were racing madly down, the movement of deer had made a clear track. At the bottom of the log the young hind made a left turn under the log and I took my chance. Leaping onto the huge trunk and launching myself into the air, I cut the distance between us and landed on the hind's midriff, bowling her over and down the hill. Both of us rolled on together and I got up first securing her to the ground while I reached for my knife to finish the job.

It was a risky thing to have done alone in the bush. Injury was a real possibility and I could have been a real problem to Chris, who may have had to wait long into the dark for my return. At least he did know where I had gone.

But now the problem was to find my rifle that was some hundreds of yards above me, leaning against a tree that I had not really taken note of. No worries, I thought. But I couldn't find it. I went back to where I had first seen the deer, but somehow it didn't look the same. I tried to find the spot where it had stood looking at me over the leaves of the tree. But no. The evening was really closing in now. I couldn't go back to the hut telling Chris that I had lost my rifle!! At walking pace in the bush, I discovered, you unconsciously memorize so much of it, but when running you don't. That's why I couldn't find the rifle now.

Finally there was only one thing for it. I went back to the deer's tailess and backsteakless body and began to backtrack the whole chase, which I probably should have done in the first place. The chase was not hard to follow. My bootprints gauged out half of the hillside in places and I was amazed at the places that I had negotiated at speed. Some of my footprints were an impossible distance apart. Such is the ability of youth, now some twenty eight years ago. The tracks of the chase took me straight back to my rifle and was I glad to see it. I had been searching for it for three-quarters of an hour. I can't imagine how a culler could ever account for having lost his rifle!

At Home in the Hills

I arrived back at the hut not long after dark to a meatless Chris but a roaring fire and a good feed. Chris was great around the camp.

CULLING

We'd come past the base and over the Mokai saddle,
To my first sight of Ohutu ridge and the Maropea straddle.
Down to the river and up to the hut Otukota,
In the evening I went up the ridge for a hunt,
Where a spiker broke from the scrub with a grunt,
I snapped off a shot with instinct not blunt
And he rolled to my feet, his tail for my deer culling quota.

A venison leg hung 'neath a beech tree shaded,
As we hunted the range till the days were well jaded.
One evening I nipped downstream midst the splash,
Climbed a prominent outcrop over the river,
Three hinds on a slip, one fell with a quiver,
The other two ran, one a survivor.
The last one fell too and it came down the cliff with a crash.

We went up the river to the hut at Maropea Forks,
Chris took the river and I climbed the ridge, evening stalks.
I heard a noise 'neath the ancient red beeches,
Fired at a face looking over the leaves,
Jaw and leg broken, he's off through the trees,
A reckless chase down the steep slope, him and me.
A leap, a tackle, it's over, my hunting knife reaches.

The tails were growing on my piece of string
As day after day home my tokens I'd bring.

The Odd Few Deer

> Each one an emblem of heroic deeds,
> How we conquered the mountains and precipice face,
> Outwitted the wily red deer in their place
> While at night by the fire we wrestled with gigantic feeds.

THREE ON THE MANGAOHANE

It had been an on and off sort of a day on the beautiful expanse of the Mangaohane Plateau, and Dennys and I had had a successful day of sorts. It had been some time since I had ended my time as a deer culler, but I still knew the guys on the block and so we shot what deer we saw, tailing them and leaving the tails in the food cupboards to help them out. It was a good way to get Dennys out of the mechanic's bay at International Harvester in Palmerston North and ensure that he retained his high country citizenship.

A long range shot at a stag on the edge of Round Bush, from the point known as Scar had spooked a mob of five hinds on a huge tussock face and we had knocked a few of them over too.

Across the golden slopes, undulating in all directions about us, it had rained off and on that February day leaving the sweet accentuated smell of the tussock drifting to us from its drenched and bowing blades, taking us to a level of contentment no city slicker will ever know. As the evening wore on we made camp under a massive rock where hard dry ground told us the rain never reached. We were collecting some firewood and stacking it against the rock, where the light breeze wouldn't blow the soon to be manufactured smoke in our faces, when several hundred feet below in a little grassy clearing beside a small creek I spotted a deer. We were already tired from the long day on the hill we had given ourselves.

The binoculars revealed that it was a young stag. Dennys wasn't keen to go all that way so I grabbed my BSA Hunter 7mm. - now mounted with the 4 power Pecar scope that had been on several

At Home in the Hills

of my rifles, and had the dents and worn silver parts to prove it – and wandered off down the tussock gully and into the tea-tree leading to the distant deer. Fifteen minutes later found me slowly approaching the clearing. The tea-tree was hanging heavily with the build up of drops from the light rain that has fallen in the late afternoon. The long, lush green grass was also soaked and had soaked my socks, which quickly transferred the moisture down into the toes of my boots. I was wet through. But a deer was near.

There was a large rock in the clearing, and, from our vantage point high above, I had noted that the deer should be about fifty yards on the far side of it. The long grass hung from my side of the clearing over into the still water of the creek, nearly brushing the grass hanging over from the other side. This lush grass of the clearing pushed up the slopes twenty of thirty yards on either side of the creek into the tea-tree barrier that receded up and away over the ridges out of view.

Three Stags on the Mangaohane (1969).

The Odd Few Deer

Somewhere up there, Dennys would undoubtedly be watching with his binoculars. Peering round the rock cautiously, I spied the deer still feeding, practically unmoved from the spot where I had first spotted it. Down went the bolt, up came the rifle, down went the deer, up came a shout from Dennys high above.

Suddenly, out of the bush on the slope to my left, raced a bigger stag down to the creek at full speed. The bolt crashed back and forward pushing another one hundred and fifty grain round forward as the stag leapt the stream, careering into the toitois at the edge of the tea-tree on the far side. He came into focus in my scope for a split second, and my firing coincided with my awareness of a third stag now racing down from the scrub where the second stag had come from. I yanked the bolt back, forgetting the shot just taken but vaguely aware that there was no movement from the toitois. The bolt came right out of the rifle! "What? My rifle's broken. How did that happen?" The stag was crossing the creek in a panicked leap. Fumbling around with the bolt, I finally realized what had happened, got the bolt back where it should be and rammed another round into the chamber. The deer was nearly gone. Dennys was yelling for me not to shoot, for the only deer he had seen was well dead. He couldn't see the other two.

The next shot got the third deer in the hip setting it up for a killing shot to the shoulder and it rolled down the hill. All over in a few seconds. In the toitois the bigger stag lay cleanly shot. I called out to Dennys that I had shot three and asked him to bring the camera.

We had our venison cooked on green tea-tree rods over a fire that evening, as the light rain that had come and gone all day finally moved on to the east. It left us peaceful in the quiet stillness, where everything hangs limp with the weight of fine rain droplets waiting for the next day when the sun will dry it all out. It was probably the fastest bit of accurate shooting that I ever did, and I lay in my sleeping bag that night under a rock very pleased with myself. Putting it with the shot that I had pulled off in the morning in the Round Bush, where a running stag had not quite outrun another piece of lead as it rounded a large beech tree thirty yards away at a speed that a greyhound would have been proud of - it had been a good day.

I slept well that night considering the hard ground and limited space over my head from the rock that we were under. I've never considered myself a really good shot but every so often I've surprised even myself.

The Unknown Stag

Dennys whispered to me that he was going to sneeze, so I lifted the smooth hollowed out cow's horn that hung around my neck on a length of cord and, fitting it to my lips, let out a low moan to drown out his stifled sneeze. Instantly a massive bellow echoed back through the tall virgin bush of the Unknown Valley, bouncing off the tall timber and multiplying itself as it crashed back at us from all angles. Again, and then again, this stag nearby sucked in air hard, pumping his lungs to exploding point and then releasing it violently, adding the wild and angry tones of his full maturity that roared out of his throat to challenge the very existence of all living things. The volume that reverberated from back in the mystery of a tangled vegetation, stretching from ground level to seventy odd feet above us, caused the hair on the nape of my neck to twist awkwardly passing on the tenseness that the rest of my body was feeling.

The bush was intensely silent then with every bird and insect in the vicinity holding its breath, as were Dennys and I. The electrical air of challenge created by a mature red stag in full-blown rut is one of the wonders of the wild, and I pity those who haven't heard it in a proper setting.

The Odd Few Deer

This trip began five days before when Dennys, the best hunting mate anyone could want, and I left our car on the bush edge near the Triplex Creek which was now over the Main Ruahine Range and some twelve hours of continuous hard walking from here. We had stopped with the possums overnight at the unkempt and dingy Upper Maropea Hut, set on a unique terrace high on the slopes of Armstrong Saddle before coming on down to the hut at Maropea Forks.

We followed the river that eases along its length providing pleasant travel most of the way. The New Zealand Forest Service built the hut in a beautiful setting here, and I love that area as only a hunter can. The hut is a place where the ghosts of hunters of a bygone era still maintain ownership.

We'd shot three stags up until now over the days of hunting behind us, but they'd only been six pointers which we had tailed for Terry, mentioned earlier, who was still contract hunting the block. Only one had been roaring, and, although not very enthusiastic, we had been able to lure it up to about fifteen feet from us before dispatching it. We did have plenty of the best cuts of venison and were putting loads of it into our meals so as to conserve our supplies. After carrying sixty-pound packs for two days we weren't too keen on just sitting down and eating it all.

The morning had dawned fine and clear with just a gentle breeze pushing the few white clouds across our limited view of the sky. As it had been blowing a strong westerly and raining more often than not over the last few days, we decided to head up the track to the north of the hut and travel on to the Unknown Tentcamp site some miles to the north to see how the stags were roaring there.

We'd seen three deer so far that day. They were on the ridge in the chest high snow grass that sprouted from the ground beneath the high level beeches, where the ground was as soaked as a sponge yet still held its shape until a careless foot turned it into an ice-skate. The first stag and hind had been too fast for us as they dashed across our view of the winding track ahead and over the side of the ridge at a fast rate of knots. The third was a nice yearling which collected two bullets. We had the back steaks in our packs for tea.

Dennys on the Mangaohane Plateau looking across to Black Hill (1968).

After the initial climb from Maropea Forks which is reasonably steep and steady, although not very high, the track follows the ridge westward and then branches off to the north gradually descending to the Unknown stream in the distance. While quietly strolling down the lower part of this ridge where the trees are tallest, minding our business, following the track just thinking of getting to the Tentcamp for a brew, a mighty roar boomed through the treetops and stopped us shaking in our boots. It was as if we had innocently walked right under the nose of a giant ogre of a stag mad at the whole universe, and he was going to take it out on us. Never had either of us heard anything like that before. He must have been only yards from us to have made such a voluminous noise we mistakenly thought.

Eyes wide as saucers we communicated with each other by a mutual stare. Packs were silently lowered, rifles checked and fingers pointed to where we guessed he would be and the possible routes of approach indicated. The bush was as thick as any you wouldn't want to enter. I cautiously raised the cows horn to my lips and moaned a half-hearted reply that sounded like a mouse's response in relation to what we had just heard. What happened then is a most beautiful memory. The volume that stag emitted was almost unbelievable. His deep guttural tones blasted out of him with the energy of a locomotive bursting out of a tunnel. Some of the air came out of his throat in frustrated hisses, too powerfully to have activated his voice box and sounded like a hundred fire extinguishers before the voice box finally caught. The magnificent sound echoed and re-echoed around us. I think that Dennys and I had pure adrenaline running through our blood streams.

We began to move in towards him. Rifles held in both hands. Minds conscious of every twig or leaf by which we might betray our position to him. For about thirty minutes we crept, slid, climbed and crawled toward him amazed at the continuous display of thunderous roaring that we were experiencing.

We moved through the more difficult places to traverse quietly when he roared, and many bushes and fallen logs that were covered with bushlawyer and nettles to hamper our progress saw two sets of wide eyes slowly emerge over them as we explored the way ahead. It always sounded as if he was just over or around the next obstacle.

Then he was silent for some time. The pollen, rising from the tangles of bracken fern that we were slowly crushing to bypass, began to tickle Dennys' nose and he urgently whispered to me that he was going to sneeze. That's where this story started. Well, after he'd finished that particular bout of roaring, grunting and bellowing that sounded more like a lion crossed with a wapiti bull than a red stag, we started towards him again. Most of the undergrowth there, as we rounded the curve of a shallow ridge heading into another wide gut, was twelve to fourteen foot high pepperwood laced with bushlawyer and under laid with nettles, so we couldn't make quiet progress quickly.

He wasn't on the far side of the next rotting tree trunk that lay down the slope of the ridge, nor was he in the next few little clearings we cautiously peered into. He wasn't under the big beech tree that stood alone out of the tangles of undergrowth that had once been a clearing. But he was somewhere near, as all this time I was continuing to moan out encouraging roars that he was beginning to get bored with although he was still answering. Finally, rounding the end of the small ridge that we had been on for the last ten minutes or so, we realized what we were on the edge of a large clearing that swept around a large concave gully only sparsely dotted with large beeches. Side by side, we edged around a pepperwood bush gaining a sweeping view of the clearing.

"There he is." Dennys whispered, loading and then raising his three oh eight rifle. I took a step to the right so as to have a better view, then looked in the direction Dennys was aiming. What a sight. About fifty yards away he stood under a large beech tree, which, casting it's shadow on him, silhouetted him against the sunlit grass and broken ground behind. He stood, not quite fully facing us but not broadside either. He was holding his nose high, looking our way, trying to catch our scent on the air; his beautifully curved antlers thrown wide on each side of his dark brown body powerfully poised in an attitude of readiness for battle. The mane about his neck was black and thick, and flowed down between his powerful shoulders and thick upper legs that bespoke only age and authority amongst his kind. What an animal. A monarch indeed.

I had but a split second to take in all the majesty and splendour of this sight because Dennys was going to fire and I didn't want to be left out of the action, but I know I'll never forget the slightest detail of that stag standing there, magnificent as he was.

I raised my rifle to my shoulder, centred on my aiming point and fired. I noticed from the corner of my awareness that Dennys' rifle recoiled as I fired, and realized we'd both fired at the same instant resulting in a single crashing explosion rolling away through the hills. The stag fell where he stood and didn't even twitch an ear as we hurried over to him. Dennys didn't know that I had fired, due to the one boom, and the fact that, although he stood a few metres to my right he was also slightly in front of me, until I stopped him and made him watch me open the bolt of my rifle and remove an empty case.

There was only one bullet hole in the stag. The way that he had dropped I thought that we had probably both hit him in the neck, but it was not so. As I was using nickel jacketed seven by fifty seven bullets, and Dennys was using his preference of copper jacketed three oh eight bullets, we had a way of knowing whose stag it was. The seven millimeter bullet was just inside the skin of the rear right leg.

The antlers weren't huge, but the trophy was.

Lying in the Unknown tent camp that night with a good feed inside me and a great mate asleep in the bunk nearby, the events of the day passed again and again through my mind. The fire that we cooked our tea on and watched into the night, as we heard two blue ducks down by the creek whistling, was dying down to a dull red glow, making it harder and harder for me to see the

At Home in the Hills

antlers propped up under the rough hand hewn table. I got up for one last look at them before lying down, closing my eyes and letting the sound of the trees growing towards the dark sky in the chill air above lull me to sleep.

Two tired hunters.

At the Unknown Tent Camp (1970).

This next poem is a fantasy but one which holds a grain of irony that all hunters feel from time to time. There is always that feeling after a fruitless day's hunting, deer have seen you and have been playing with you all the while, and you have been frustrated and physically tiring which accentuates those feelings as the day declines. Contrast that with the hope that one day, perhaps today, that dream stag will appear and you will pull of the shot of your life amidst the extra flow of sight jerking adrenaline thereby beating the trophy animal with all his years of man wariness. This is in honor of the stags that die of old age and the hunters that never give up.

THE ANCIENT STAG

Across the Mangaohane realms a tattered stag remains.
His gnarled old limbs and scarred red hide
Ghost the bush where he abides
And no hunter from any side
Has downed this stag of those domains

His antlers now don't scrape the trees
As once they used to do.
They're only spread to fifty inch
And near as long at just a pinch
Yet still the greatest head he'd cinch,
But none can sight him clear and true.

He teases all the deerstalkers that go off after him.
He leads them off to distant hills
Then doubles back to camp so still,
Leaves his mark by tents until
Exhausted hunters wander in.

His prints are often seen by tussock tops and creeks.
He wanders the open land it seems, and yet
A hunter rarely gets
A sight of him, although he lets
The unarmed trampers get some peeks.

I saw him once at half a mile, out of rifle range.
He looked at me across the way
And glibly gloated as to say
All you kind can play all day
But this is my home and to you its strange.

CHAPTER NINE
Bad Weather

TARARUA TOPS

It was a cloudy and moonless night, as black as the inside of a cow, and my brother Bob and I were following the ever-decreasing glow of inadequate torches through the murk of the track to Field Hut from the Otaki Forks car park. Pools of water hiding ankle deep mud just under the surface stretched across and along the track, making it impossible to avoid, and so sploshing through them we sucked and slurped our way from the darkness of one to the next, leaving them in the silence behind us. My pencil torch finally gave up and we continued on, with me stumbling on behind trying to remember what I had seen Bob's torch reveal in a dancing flicker moments before. My mind never seemed to get the knack of focusing on both what was being revealed and what had moments before been revealed. Each needed more concentration than I was able to muster.

We arrived at the hut in the middle of the night, mud splashed but eager. Over the next few days we planned to travel the main range via Maungahuka to the Anderson Memorial and Waitewaiwai huts. This was our second attempt at this trip; having been thwarted by the weather on the first try mentioned

At Home in the Hills

somewhere else in this book.

Morning arrived with a crash as the door of the hut burst open and three keen parka-clad youngsters poked their heads in to the slumbering interior, where moments before, we were dozing deeply in the unkeenness that only waves of wind-driven rain on the roof induces. Their keenness, not diluted at all, even pumped up perhaps by their dripping shapes, seemed to be a rebuke and a statement of superiority all wrapped up in one courteous sneer of, "Good morning! We're on our way to Vosseler and Alpha huts". The door closed and they were gone. Bob and I murmured to each other from the guilt-ridden depths of our down cocoons about the pointlessness of getting up early, as the round trip we had planned was obviously out of the question now that this weather had risen. Then we commented on the clothes that the young guys at the door had been wearing. Parkas, brushed cotton shirts, cotton shorts and the usual woolen socks and leather boots. We hoped that they had some woolen clothing for the upper parts of their bodies to put on before they got too far on the open tops that they would break out onto just above the hut.

As the morning progressed the weather didn't let up. It didn't even stay the same. The howling of the wind rocked the ancient hut and the track nearby was a running stream, cutting grooves through the earth and carrying leaves and twigs over the side of the ridge into the bush below. Visibility outside was only twenty to thirty yards in the mist. We mentioned our three early morning visitors often and wondered how they were faring. We were sure that they would stop at Vosseler Hut, as we knew it must be fair howling on the top of the range. Vosseler is gone now, as the old wreck that used to be Kime at the time of this story has since been rebuilt.

Late in the afternoon the weather abated for a few minutes, and during that time Bob and I decided to go for Vosseler. When the rain is pounding on the roof it can be hard to make the decision to leave the protection of a hut and head out into it. It took the encouragement of a tantalizing few minutes of respite in the gale for us to commit ourselves to going. Before we had our coats and packs on, the torment returned, but we had decided to go and so, shutting the door of the hut, off we went.

Away from the noise of the hut's resistance to the weather it didn't seem so bad, even good. Before long we were happily climbing around the side of Tabletop and heading over the flat to Dennen. We didn't stop all the way to Vosseler. What was there to stop for? There were no views and you only felt cold when standing still. I have found that I have often done the fastest traveling times when the weather was bad. I guess it's because the discomfort of stopping is usually worse than the discomfort of pack straps that are beginning to cut and lungs that are working hard. It is easier to take a few deep breaths with a brief pause and go on.

Leaning into the wind, heads down and faces twisted out of the full blast of the wind under balaclavas and hoods, both hands stuffed up the opposing sleeves of our parkas we gratefully stepped through the door of Vosseler.... to find it empty. Those young guys were on their way to Alpha. We sure hoped that they had other clothes, different from the ones that we saw them wearing.

The day blew on and we consoled ourselves with warm soup and cups of hot Milo that our little white spirits burner fought the cold air to produce for us. Vosseler Hut was tied down with wire ropes at the corners and we were sure glad of that that day. The night blew on. In the morning the wind had died down a lot, and even though the cloud was still down, giving the surrounding easy tussock slopes an eerie atmosphere, Bob and I plodded over to the Kime wreck for an enjoyable break from the wooden confines of the hut. There's only so much sleeping, talking and reading of the rubbishy books people carry to the hills that you can do in a stretch.

In the fairyland of cloud-covered tops a person coming towards you first appears as a mysterious smudge at the extremity of visual definition. Then he appears as a blob of gray definitely not a part of the natural scene. Then he becomes a matt gray human shape of indeterminate height because he is floating in the mist defying your ability to define distance. Suddenly he is right beside you and you are talking to him. This is exactly how we met this guy. He was dressed in gear that was new to us but was obviously ideally suited for the conditions. He seemed to be in a frame of mind that would suit the back yard on a summer's day better than this decidedly unpleasant one. He was an "experienced tramper". Something that Bob and I would not be for some time yet. Back at the hut he told us of mountaineering experiences that he had had in the Southern and European Alps. This part of the world, even in the conditions we were experiencing, was in fact just a casual jaunt for him. We were impressed.

Then he told us of three guys that he had come across on the ridge back towards Alpha the day before. They had held him up a day, and now he could only stay with us for a quick brew before heading for the Ohau river where he had to be the next day. All three of our brief acquaintances of the day before had been suffering from hypothermia. One had gone to sleep because he was feeling warm again after being cold all day. The second was sitting down off the side of the ridge and refusing to go on. He would soon have gone into a death sleep too. The third was better off and was unsuccessfully trying to get the other two to move on when our friend turned up. He made them move and got them to Alpha Hut somehow where he was able to warm them up and see them able to go on the next day.

Then he wandered off into the cloud alone, a man enjoying the hills. It made the words go through my mind from the Lone

Ranger series at the Saturday afternoon matinees at the movies: "Who was that masked man?" He saved their lives. I read about it in the paper a few days later.

Bob and I returned to complete that trip at a later date. Even then the weather was iffy. I would rather abandon a trip if I'm unsure of the weather and come back and have another go at it later than to make it my last half trip. As some mountaineer once said," You never conquer a mountain it merely lets you climb it from time to time". Hills are tougher than men. Peter Hillary's turning back on K2 a few years back when his companions carried on to their deaths is a shining example of the wisdom of adventurous caution.

FLOODED WAIOTAURU

April 1967 found two young hunters making their way over the grassy flats of a river still being released from the grip of a deadly still and moonlit night, in the Otaki Forks area. Robin Smith, one of the twins that made up the center of my friendships, and I. Our mountain mule packs clinging comfortably to our backs, the only rifle between us slung in my hand, a Parker Hale .303 Supreme, we were swinging our way over the terraces and through the river crossings to a hunting ground that was abounding in deer which seemed to have been missed by the cullers of the area.

The adrenaline in our systems, slowly rising as we had driven the hour or so from home, was still rising as the hidden creek of our discussions over the last few weeks was coming closer and closer and we excitedly noted and accentuated the goodness of everything that we saw and were experiencing. Clear blue sky just lighting the peaks over the main range to the east and the frost crunching under our feet promised an enjoyable two days hunting in the creeks and gullies of the place that we were headed.

At Home in the Hills

A few hours later the main river had closed in and we were boulder-hopping all of the time until we came to the major forks. Branching up to the left here we soon came to the side stream we were looking for. It looked just the same as so many others throughout the North Island but being on this stream at this time of the year when the stags were feeling less cautious, being side tracked with other issues, Robin's and my heart beats rose in anticipated eagerness as our boots trod what seemed to be a sacred valley. The gray rocks of the stream bed were still in deep shadow as the sun had still not penetrated into the depths of the very steep sided slopes that shot away up into the almost whiteness of a heavily contrasted sky. The cold water and brisk mountain air tempered the heat of our hard working bodies and we clambered our way on, bend after bend of the gorgy bit of the river, before it opened up further on.

Many streams do that and its appearance of forking with a larger one is often deceptive and discourages a hunter looking for a handy deer or two by the mere aggression of the immediate vicinity. One waterfall, issuing from a dark cut in steep cliffs and dropping inhospitably over mossy rocks into a lake in Fiordland, proved that to me as, after I persisted up its gorgy twisting interior for an hour or so, it broke out into park like flats under open trees and a beautiful lake into one of the most memorable day's hunting of my life.

We slowly became aware of the smell. Then on a particular bend we were hit hard with it. Goats! There was a steady light breeze in our faces and we began moving cautiously, probing the slopes and clear spots on the bush clad sides. Each bend the smell increased until it was a positive stench assailing us, causing looks of disgust to pass between us. Soon we crept into view of a huge clay slip. Lying at its feet were the remains of tall trees that had once stood full of life, now crumpled and rotting in heaps, lying in abandon over each other while the lawyers and weeds invaded their demise. The heads of two billy goats appearing over a dirt bank curiously examining us were met by a hail of lead. Suddenly goats were running everywhere and we handed the rifle back and forth, reloading in between, while the number of goats decreased in number and increased in distance. I remember that Robin finished the last one off over a hundred yards away as it looked back to see why it wasn't being followed by the others. A lot of animals make that fatal mistake.

A few years later while doing a short time with the NZFS in the Tararuas, I learned from the field officer there, Ray Wise, that the cullers then were being paid $8.50 per tail for deer and goats. I remembered this day with sorrow that I wasn't culling at the time. That was a lot of money in those days.

We were still short of our camping place and so headed on up the river, still hoping to find deer. In the second gorge a brief movement in the cutty-grass under the pungas a hundred yards ahead on the face of the next bend caught my eye. Examining the spot through the scope sight on my rifle I could see a young hind peering out from the fronds at us, unperturbed. She fell onto the rocks below at the shot and we had meat for tea. Things were beginning to go well. Now all we needed was a decent stag, the goal of the weekend.

We had decided not to take a tent as the weather was fine and didn't show any sign of breaking, and we had wanted to try our hands at bivouacing out anyway. So, when we arrived at the flat that we had been planning to camp on we set about making a shelter. We chopped through two very tall pungas about three feet up from the ground, and then leaned the fallen end of the trunk on the stumps to make a sloping beam. Against both sides we leaned heaps of long fronds from the ample supply of other pungas matted up the hillside around the edges of the clear and grassy flat. Underneath there was a narrow dark tunnel that we in our youthful ignorance thought would be weatherproof. Our sleeping bags fitted neatly there side by side. It sure looked like a great bivouac.

After building a surround of rocks not far away, we lit a fire under the shade of a clump of trees boldly standing in the centre of the flats and made a brew of tea. For the next few hours we lolled in the sun enjoying the heat of the day, the stillness of the bush, the friendly trickling of the clear ankle deep stream over sparkling rocks, and each other's companionship in the solitude of the bush. We were anxious for the middle of the day to pass so that we could explore upstream in the late afternoon when the deer were likely to be moving about again. Several brews, spaced an hour or so apart, were downed with cubes of spit roasted fresh venison, heavily salted. Idly wandering down to the water's edge and back we passed the day. It was remarkably still and we commented on it several times. I now get wary when that kind of stillness wafts in to camp.

About four o'clock we geared up and as the sky quietly clouded over, without affecting the stillness of the valley, we headed on upstream, climbing over some log jams and scaling one particular waterfall that had a huge tree trunk leaning against making a smooth bleached ladder for our use. The six-foot scramble from its roots over the lip of the falls amidst the shower of water descending on us presented a challenging moment but we were soon away again. Two more billy goats trotted over the rocks in front of us and we just watched them go off into the bush, unwilling to upset the valley with any more shots. We were hoping for a stag. We were not to be disappointed.

It was only a small creek by this time as we had traveled a long way up it and the crossings were able to be leapt across. The steepness of the bouldery riverbed had increased and I was leading Robin by ten or so yards. After making our way up the shingle face of a bare, loose metal terrace we picked a path across its elevated plain through the dried sticks of treetops that had been covered and killed by this stone avalanche, which had come down in some past horrendous storm.

Glancing back over the terrace to check Robin's progress, I could see beyond him and down into a portion of the stream that the terrace had hidden, and there beside the water, clear, sharp and magnificent, stood a wonderful stag. He stood side on, but was looking straight at us, having been alerted to us at the same moment that I had seen him - and his head was high, his black antlers held regally angling over his shoulders. The deep red coat was still visible over his ribs but his neck, legs, belly and ridge of his spine were black, contrasting wonderfully with the bleached white of the rocks he was standing amongst and the greeny gray of the water near his feet. It was a sight. It is etched in my memory now still as clear as then. MAGNIFICENT! A memory worth a million dollars. A wild stag in a wild place.

My eyes must have been nearly out of my head as Robin, seeing the look on my face turned and saw the stag as well. He began to race towards me as he was in my line of fire and I could do nothing until he was behind me. The beautiful stag turned, tilting his nose up when the weight of his antlers jerked his head back as he ran.

Back around the terrace he came, below where we had just been, and then he turned for the bush up near us where he had obviously walked out from not long before. My first shot went low into a log that he was running behind where only his head and spine showed above it. As he quartered towards us I fired again too fast and the shot went who knows where. Then he turned directly away from us to make the leap up off the terrace into the bush proper and I knew that I had him. As he leapt up and away, he exposed his whole spine to a shot down on his back and the bullet killed him instantly. He slid to the ground and we quickly approached.

We stood in silence for a moment or two trying to emotionally catch up with the adrenaline enhanced actions we had just been performing. Then the talk came in excited bursts. For us it was a trophy head. The colors of that stag and his antlers were a wonder to us youngsters. He was the essence of the wild captured and made our own. Not captured by his physical death but in a mystical way that only the hunter knows. A capturing that takes the whole environment, the meaning of the mountains and the essence of wilderness right into his soul changing him and molding his very existence around that which is captured. That day was, and is still, a treasure.

Back at our campsite we ate our tea of kebabbed venison in the growing dimness of the evening hastened by a cloud darkened sky. Our firelight lit the trees about the small flat falling on the antlers, which drew our eyes constantly, enhancing the day's adventures, but the uncanny stillness continued and began to have an ominous presence. If I had known then what I know now, we would have headed out of there even in the dark. At nine o'clock it began to rain lightly and we headed for the seclusion of our punga bivvy and sleeping bags. Soon we were off in the satisfied land of nod. Successful hunters of the elusive red stags in the wild and rambling mighty Tararua Ranges. Heroes of little boy's dreams.

The rain didn't stop. It steadily fell in increasing volumes. I now know that when rain starts slowly and increases slowly then it will probably really set in. This was that kind of rain. By midnight it was heavy and I began to wonder about the creek's potential level at daylight. At some unearthly hour of the morning, I awoke to find that my feet were in a puddle of water, while still in my

Bad Weather

sleeping bag. It was soaked from the knees down and a fine mist was floating all about us. Robin and I never woke at the same time in the night but were both aware and concerned about the stream. We listened to it throughout the night but didn't notice any rising of its sound.

The morning emerged from the night as perceptible as a black cat emerging from a coal bin on a moonless night. We watched but never saw it come. It held as much prospect of a good day as a firing squad does of a picnic and we hurriedly packed up in the heavy raindrops falling vertically, so thick it was a wonder there was any breathable air between them. My sleeping bag was soaked but Robin had had a waterproof sleeping bag cover so his was still mostly dry. The stream was still running clear and had not risen above its normal level. Ankle deep at the crossing places.

With no delay we headed down river with some legs of venison each and the antlers draped over my pack. Not worrying about the drenching we were getting our feet moved as fast as possible and our mouths not at all. We knew we had to put all effort into getting out of the hills and onto the farm land. However the rain caught us.

Our splashing across the stream soon became knee high wading through it. It slowly discoloured into an orange and white flow; bouncing around the rocks and swirling the pools that had minutes before been clear and still. Soon we were waist-deep in the crossings and linking arms to hold each other up in the torrent. The river became a roaring wildness between the steep slopes of a typically remote Tararua creek. Then we turned back only one third the way across a particular crossing. It was too swift and I thought it was dangerous. Anyway, I said to Robin, if we do cross here and are unable to make another crossing then we will be on the wrong side and unable to reach the farmland until the river goes down. That may be days away. On the west side that we were on, we had the option of sidling above the river and still making it out. On the other side we would eventually come to the major forks and be blocked in between the two rivers not able to go downstream anymore. It was time to start sidling.

The steep sides of the stream made sidling above it a very up and down affair. At one time we would be on the riverbed and soon after would have to climb two hundred feet above it to get over a bluff that fell into the river from high above. The supplejack creepers added to the frustration, and the heavy rain that continued all day slowly drained us emotionally, as well as causing the floor of the forest to slime up and become an obstacle course of treacherous footing. We slipped, slid, climbed, sidled, fell, sat, rose again, plodded on and on and on all day. Eating dry bread for lunch caused the roof of our mouths to hurt and the only thing that we didn't lack was drink. The rain running down off our heads not only satisfied our thirst continuously, but also filled our eyes, causing us to endlessly wipe them and try to wring our hair to give us a moment of time when we could see normally. Rain, rain, rain all the time. Heavy, heavy rain. After that experience I've come to value the wide brimmed hat. It keeps your eyes dry better than any coat hood can.

We noticed the slip where we had shot the mob of goats the day before and on we went. After a time we discarded the legs of venison. Getting out before dark arrived became the priority and our energy resources were depleting fast. Then I propped the antlers against a tree and, taking one last look left them there. I guess they are still there.

The valley was filled with cloud and visibility was less than one hundred yards. We didn't know how far down the valley we were but all we could do was box on with the assurance that each step we took wouldn't have to be done again and so progress was being made.

Bad Weather

In the frustration of the day and in the mental searching for a way to ensure we would get out before the day was over, I came up with the bright idea of climbing over the ridge to the west of us and dropping into the stream on the other side that ran out onto farm land nearer the car park. It was a smaller stream, having a much smaller watershed, and so couldn't get as flooded as the one that we were following.

We decided to give it a go and so up we went, further and further into the peasoup of cloud and the maelstrom of violent wind and waving trees. The bush slowly changed as we climbed higher. The mosses of altitude appeared and the bush became clearer underneath. The high trees of the valleys gave way to the shorter trees of higher altitude on exposed ridges, and finally we hit the hard winds that we knew would be blowing at the top of the ridge where the westerly weather arrived unhindered from the Tasman Sea. Although we could only see a few yards now we surmised that we had to be on the main dividing ridge between the two watersheds because of the strength of the wind. So we crossed the top and began the descent.

Slipping and sliding it seemed a long way to the bottom. Finally we could make out the bush on the other side of the valley as a faint color change in the cloud. Then the individual trees could be seen dropping to meet the ridge that we were on. Finally we could see the stream below and noticed that we were opposite a big slip in the river. It looked familiar. With bitter disappointed it dawned on us where we had seen it before. It was in fact the same slip where we had shot the goats the day before. We could see some of them still lying there. We were back in the same river. Even worse. We were back upstream from where we had begun to climb over to the other watershed.

What we had thought was the main ridge top was only a side ridge of it and we had merely crossed into another part of the same valley. We sat down very disappointed and weary. The loss of those two hours was very demoralizing. We now doubted whether we could make it out before the complete darkness of night in a storm arrived, which we knew would arrive early.

At five thirty we cut down another punga and made as good a shelter as our weary bodies allowed. We had made the main river and it was wide, brown and flashing west in great mounding rapids that were way beyond crossing. We had found a small terrace not far from the riverbank and as my sleeping bag was saturated we wriggled and squirmed into the one bag under the shelter. Our parkas and everything plastic that we could find were spread over the bivouac to create as much waterproofing as possible. We had sighted five deer as we had stumbled, crawled and slid our way through the bush that day, but had no interest in them except to watch them move off when they saw us. They hadn't even seemed spooked, as any self-respecting deer should have been, and we put it down to the fact that they were just as bent on survival as we were.

As we lay there with the rain falling, we listened to the roaring river and wondered what the next day would bring and how our parents were handling the fact that we hadn't arrived home as expected. It wasn't a comfortable night but it was at least warm. Two in one sleeping bag assured that. Luckily we were carrying no extra weight or we wouldn't have fitted. We woke each other up all the time during the night as we moved and needed to turn over. You can only imagine what that was like and how long it took us.

At one point during the long black hours I woke and lifted my head to see of there was any light outside the inadequate shelter we had hurriedly made. My head made a splash as I lifted it. Again it splashed as I put it down again. It was resting in a puddle of mud. In the morning I had to clean a pad of mud about twenty

Bad Weather

millimeters thick off the right side of my head.

Dawn was finally there when I opened my eyes for what seemed like the thousandth time. It was not the kind of dawn you really appreciate. It was only just there. A shade lighter than the night, but with all the characteristics of night still remaining. The best way I can think of to describe its arriving is to say that the day squirmed its way into a meager existence with the grandeur of a slug being squashed under your boot. It was still raining and I could hear the river rolling past on its impatient way to the sea. We got up. I'm sure that it was only the excessive tiredness of the previous day's exertions that had allowed us to sleep most of that night, yet, even standing, my body felt none of the aliveness of being awake. It was Monday morning and we sloshed out to the river to see how it looked. The water level was definitely down a couple of feet from the night before, even though the rain had not let up all night and was still falling if not quite so heavily.

We had a half of a sausage each for breakfast and even that we had to force ourselves to eat. We just weren't hungry. Then we packed up and headed off downstream. At a wide place where the river seemed to be reasonably shallow, although still brown and moving at a fair speed, we ventured out to see how far across we could get. Linked together with a strong grip of each others forearms we angled downstream. As the water level passed our navels our feet began to drift along the stones on the bottom but we continued to make progress across the current and finally scrambled up the stones on the other side.

Four hours later at ten o'clock our worried parents received a relieving phone call which a farmer had let us make from his phone in the passage of his home. I'm not sure that I would let a person as wet as we were into my house like they did for us. Our parents later said that they weren't really worried about our not turning up as planned, knowing that we had our heads screwed on well. If they hadn't been worried I don't know why not, because I certainly was at times.

It had been a pretty rough weekend. One to remember for wonderful times and one to remember for tough times. The first day was a dream come true. the second was a dream come true too. A nightmare.

Late Monday afternoon found me back at work in the endless bracken fern country behind the pretty township of Motuoapa on the shores of Lake Taupo. I was at that time working with a survey party of the Lands and Survey Dept. on a land swap between the Hautu Prison Farm and Tuwharetoa Maori lands. As we left work that evening for the welcome bunks of the Motuoapa Motels we could hear the moans and groans of stags roaring on the slopes of the Waimarino River that wound its way up to the drawing heights of Ngapuketurua. I made myself a promise that I would go there one day and have a crack at those stags and that magnetic land too. Tough times in the hills can soon be forgotten when the sound of stags roaring fills your ears and haunts your soul again. It was however some years before I was able to fulfill that promise to myself.

Ruahine Storm

It had been a wild and noisy night under the inadequate shelter of the aged and dilapidated tent camp in the middle reaches of the Waikamaka River. Rain, hail and rising winds were announcing the beginnings of a Ruahine storm that ended up bringing much damage to the middle of the North Island during the end of 1968. Chris Satherley and I had been contract hunting our way around the Hikurangi block over the past weeks and were due out at the Mokai Base for tail count in two days. We woke to hail landing on our sleeping bags, some eight feet from the crack it came in by, between the canvas and pole door and the pole that

Bad Weather

would be called a lintel in a building of greater dignity. As the door was only six feet high at the most, the hail was attaining quite an oblique angle from the wind that puffed and blew the canvas like the sail of an America's Cup yacht coming about.

A few weeks later we returned and rebuilt that camp with new canvas and poles. Due to government ideas of economy that new camp was torn down before it was able to have a decent go at surviving a Ruahine storm of its own, and a small hut called Wakelings was built there in the early seventies.

I was glad that I didn't have to visit the loo that morning as the one there was a six foot wide, eight foot long and six foot deep hole with a single beech pole suspended the length of it just out over the edge to lean on while doing business. There was no roof, walls or floor other than what nature provided and the hail was vicious that morning. As all dead timber is apt to do the pole over the hole was subject to rot and over the years the substance in the bottom of the hole became increasingly alarming. It took a lot of courage to lean out over that particular, hellish chasm.

One day, of course, the pole broke without warning and the hapless individual who remains nameless had nothing to grasp to save himself. The hole was eight feet long and leaping to the side was not possible. Down he went. It was after many washes in the creek before he was even fit for the society of the usually not notably clean cullers he was with. As I said, I was glad that I didn't have to pay a visit there this particular morning.

Chris was a very rugged, fit and strong outdoors type, well-built with a shock of reddish hair and a simple brusk way of expressing himself that left no doubt of his meanings. He was first up this morning and in no time had a fire blazing. As the fireplace was right beside the door which didn't stop much of the weather blasting, in and as the chimney was of rotting and dilapidated logs, he had to stand and take a lot of the weather while igniting the dead beech leaves under the chips and twigs collected from the chopping block the night before. There's nothing like a decent fire to cook on, and it was during my time culling that I learned to do it well. Watching people poking little twigs into tiny gaps of a toy teepee six inches high that has a sprig of smoke coming from it and a flicker of flame fooling about under it I realize the value of firelighting knowledge.

The key to lighting a good fire is to have lots of flammable dead leaves and twigs that will burn in a large flame and pile on that a lot of bigger twigs that are burnable so that you get a big blaze of twigs maybe three to four feet high. Around that place four large logs in a square that will reflect the heat back into the base of the fire. Then lay your bigger split timber criss cross over that in two to three layers keeping each layer of logs parallel with an inch or so between them to allow air to get down into the depths. Before the first flare of flame has died down, you can have the billy boiled and the fire is ready to cook a three course meal. You'll be eating before the gas primus guys have boiled their first water. When you have finished they'll take over your fire and ten minutes later they'll be back on their primuses because they have destroyed the fire either by putting the wrong type of wood on it or by laying good wood on it in a way that it cannot burn properly.

Chris suggested, without any argument from me, that we eat quickly, pack up and move out in the hope of getting past Otukota hut to the bridge and up over the Mokai Saddle before the river rose and forced us out over the tops of the Mokai Patea Range. Not a happy place to have to travel in this weather.

We were soon well fed with about twelve weetbix each, soaked in a rich mixture of milk powder and cold water and coated with spoonfuls of sugar followed by a feed of venison steaks from a well hung black leg suspended in the safe and vegetables from a tin. Any young man eats as if he is trying to physically fill up his whole body, legs and all, but we who were living and climbing the hills all day in the weather and demands of the bush ate a hang of a lot more than average. Especially as we usually only had two feeds a day. Some of us went into a restaurant, one time, eating our way through the menu twice. And none of us had an ounce of fat on us either.

Parka'd up with every zip and dome fastened to its fullest we bade goodbye to protection for the next four to five hours. The hail struck our bare legs like an attack from a hundred slug guns. Our heads were bowed down so that the hail couldn't hit our faces and our hands were as far up the sleeves of our parkas as possible, yet some of our fingers still were punished for being exposed curling around the stocks of our rifles.

As we moved out from the slight shelter of the trees onto the river bed proper I'm sure that some demon of the weather grinned a malicious sneer. We raced for the water and waded into the icy stuff that turned our legs red instantly being however grateful that the hail couldn't get our legs there. For the next hour or so, while the hail continued to scour the valley, we spent as much time as possible in water wading downstream even though the temperature of the water was only a little above freezing. Our legs went numb but because of the fast pace we were keeping we felt warm with the exertion. It was an exhilarating time as can often be the case in harsh weather.

Slowly the river rose and equally slowly discolored but we were racing over the distance with the surefootedness only those who have spent continuous months in the hills can do. Chris was in front of me most of the way and I was hard put to keep up with that capable and well built figure. He would plow through a crossing waist deep with foaming waves rushing between the giant rocks and sweeping around the next bend himself being swept along as he diagonally dogged his way to the other side. Not looking back he would spring on over the stones leading to the next crossing, leaving me to follow his example without hesitation or be left where I stood. It was a race against the storm and we were well suited to the task. It was a wonderful thing to be as fit and well-tuned to the elements as we were that day. The rocks of the river bed and cliffs that appeared so friendly when the sun basked on them turned to glowering faces frowning at us from all sides and slippery mazes that were coldly disappointed not to be able to hinder us more as we passed on. The clear water that would twinkle at us as it gurgled out a cheery good day on a nice day had turned into a cold killer that challenged us to a greater duel of horrors at each crossing. Yet we had it all licked so far and were, in my mind at least, enjoying the battle.

At one point we had to climb up over a rocky bank onto a bush covered terrace as the river had blocked the usual crossing with a particularly angry cauldron of water and hand holds were few. Balancing good foot holds, we grasped tiny plants that would never have held our weight but did assist our balance long enough to get us over the lip and away again downstream. Go-go-go, onward we raced the rising river.

At the back of our minds was the thought of what the river would be like below the forks where the Maropea river that joined the Waikamaka just upstream from Otukota Hut. With the joining of that river, which had a large watershed, the crossings could become impossible. We knew that we could stay at Otukota but the river was a bit gorgy at the forks and not easy to climb out of if possible at all. However when we arrived at the forks we found that the Maropea was still running clear and low, and even though there was a rising with its added volume we were able to continue.

We popped up to Otukota hut for five minutes and I downed a

tin of cold spaghetti while Chris had something that I was too busy to note well. We couldn't hang around there getting cold with the inactivity, while the river rose below us so back down to the river we went and on downstream we walked, swam, floated and ran.

Rounding one of the last bends I saw the only possible crossing place quietly roaring its challenge to us, and I must confess I didn't think that we could do it. However Chris didn't hear my request to link arms as we crossed. The wind and rain whisked my words away into the torment around us and scattered them across a thousand acres of gale lashed slopes where a million trees screamed out their response to the storm that was getting its fury vented as it crossed the central ranges.

Without so much as a flicker of hesitation, Chris plunged into the river with the bottom half of his pack under the water and his rifle held out in a hand that was waving about over his head, helping give ballast to the changing centre of gravity occurring because of the moving surface under his feet. He was being swept away by the current of water but was still making some progress towards the other side. I waited to see his fate. He was into the beginnings of the rapids proper which thundered away dropping ten or so feet over the next fifty into a deep swirling hole under a black cliff before he got a firm footing again and I could see him steadying and walking out the far side. He didn't so much as look back but kept on to the next bend in the river.

After only hesitating twice I plunged in. Crisis brings it own concentration and I was soon beyond any feelings of doubt. My body was leaning and straining forward as the water level rose up above my midriff and I could feel my pack begin to float behind me. My legs were windmilling below the water as they swiped the bottom of the river at each passing pushing me a little bit forward towards the far side even as I was being swept downstream. For each two feet I was being swept downstream I reckoned that I was making one foot across or maybe six inches. Anyway I was getting across. The rapids were coming up fast and my legs were doing about five hundred revs a minute. Finally I struck the bottom firmly and was climbing up the other side as Chris had done. I was out and swinging along with a grin on my face. It strikes me now how strangely unusual it seems to be, at the same time having such a ball walking down that river that day while also being worried and at times scared.

Jim Warren on the Otupaes (1969).

Bad Weather

We made the track to the Mokai Saddle without anymore hairy bits and once over the saddle a thousand feet above were soon taking off our wet gear at the door of the Mokai Base while a very welcome cuppa was being poured out for us inside by Jim Warren who too had arrived for the tail count rendezvous, but a day earlier.

The damage from that storm made national news and many roads were closed due to landslides, fences were destroyed from flooding and there were stock losses as well. I thought it had been a lot of fun.

There have been lots of times when bad weather has made an impression on me. There was the time in the Wapiti River when it rained. We had tied the dinghy up at the head of Lake Thomson dragging it onto the dry edge and fastening the rope six feet up the trunk of a substantial tree. The rain had, to use the old cliche that doesn't do the reality justice this time, fair bucketed down all night. It was impossible to hear each other speak in the hut as the sound of the rain on the roof was literally deafening. We would put our mouths within an inch of each other's ears and yell to be understood.

The waterfall near the hut was an addition to the general bombardment of decibels. Someone should have complained to the local authorities because I'm without doubt the noise was beyond healthy levels and someone should have been sent an official letter. When we went down to the lake the next day, observing the thousands of waterfalls that had appeared on the hillsides falling out of the clouds above its south and west vertical barriers, we found that we had to swim out to the boat and dive down six feet underwater to untie the rope that was threatening to pull its the bow beneath the surface. The stern of the boat was jutting up out of the water and the bow was within inches of submersion. The lake had risen twelve feet overnight and it is not a small lake, taking half an hour to row the length of it.

At Home in the Hills

Bad weather. Sometimes bad weather can be wonderful weather. Sometimes fine weather can be a real pain and a bore. Good weather is the right kind of weather for the situation that you find yourself in. It's best not to think of bad and good weather but to find the best of each as they occur and add it to the overall enjoyment instead of letting it detract from the time in the hills that you have. One thing I can guarantee. As the years roll on it will be the bad weather that you have experienced that you will talk about and remember most. It does have its enjoyment even if it's sometimes only in retrospect.

Chapter Ten
One Day in Fiordland

The tent was a good place to wake up in. The day before, nine of us had left Thomson Hut on its lake edge and had made our way up to Lake Sutherland, where in a small clear spot on the western edge, we had sat down together for the last time for several days to enjoy a brew. The tussock tops towered above us on all sides, appearing through the tree tops as we had made ground in single file up the flatness of the glacier-carved river bottom. Through an opening made possible by the small clearing of hunters' camp, they were now caught in solid view over the lakes stillness and their inspiration was sharply etched against a clear blue sky.

Sutherland Lake is a jewel in a magnificent setting and the campsite that we sat in held an exciting history for any hunter. Here, massive antlers of the biggest round horned deer in the world had been triumphantly brought into the camps of yesteryear, trophies of one of the most inhospitable and inaccessible back country areas in the world.

We sat in small, excited groups as we ate chunks of chocolate and downed the strong brew of tea that was handed around from one enthusiastic young hunter to another. It was only the second day of a ten day trip and we were yet to see a deer. From that point we broke up into groups of three. The two that I had been allotted to go with were named John Muir and Rodger someone. His surname has gone from my memory I am afraid, but I do remember that he was very keen on shotgun shooting and had won some important trophies for it. We packed up and returned back down the path that we had just walked for a small distance to the fork of Rum Gully and then made our way into its gorgy beginnings. Immediately, we began to see fresh deer sign here and there as we picked our way over and around the mossy rocks and under the moss draped trees. Everything was drooling with mosses of every kind it seemed. Moss on the rocks. Moss on the tree trunks. Moss hanging from the branches. Moss hanging from the moss that hung from the branches. What a wonder world it was. Finally we broke out of the gorgy beginnings of the valley, and the terraces that we traveled became wider and the deer trails deepened and showed much use. John and Rodger had been walking in front of me and I was all wide-eyed and eager, looking at every new thing that this land revealed.

We all had heavier packs on than I was accustomed to for a ten day hunting trip, but then I was not used to including luxuries like legs of bacon, loaves of bread, milk and the like in the hills. However the previous years of meat hunting had prepared me well and the walking was nevertheless easy compared to what I was used to. It was basically flat on the old glacial valley floors and a sixty pound pack had no comparison to a one hundred and eighty pound deer carcass. I had carried, with some help getting to my feet, a two hundred and sixty seven pound one for an hour or so once. Still have the receipt from Consolidated Traders to prove it.

The valley opened up we began to look for the clearing that

One Day in Fiordland

we had been told about by John Anderson who had organized the whole culling trip for the N.Z. Deerstalkers Association that we were a part of. We were here to shoot females only so as to prove to the New Zealand Forest Service that the N.Z.D.A. could administer and control the Wapiti area. Unfortunately they were not impressed and within a few years helicopters were decimating the herd from the air.

Suddenly over the tops of my two comrades' heads I spotted the red coat and gray velvet antlers of a stag thirty yards away, feeding in the park-like greenery of the bush. Hissing to get the attention of my friends who had been watching the progress of their feet more than the surrounding bush, and without alerting the stag, I pointed out the unaware animal in front of us. Quickly and quietly packs were slipped off shoulders and eyes that were simply slogging out the trail became wide and intense as cameras were fitted to telephoto lenses and we crept into good positions for some photos.

Several shots were taken before one S.L.R. camera clanged too loudly and the stag, or should I say bull, raised his head and moved off into the drapes with the movement that only a much larger animal than a red stag could perform. From that moment a stag and a bull became different animals to me. The proportions aren't much different between the two but the movement of the much larger animal is so distinctive as the timing of pace seems slower in the bull but the speed over the ground is markedly faster. He truly ghosted away pausing for one last color slide shot from John that turned out to be very frameable.

As we burst out into the clearing that we were to camp in we caught one last sight of this twelve point bull as he disappeared into the trees, high on the other side of the creek from us up towards the bluffs that climbed vertically away to the blue sky and hid the ridge tops over the distant curve of their altitude.

At Home in the Hills

We crossed the creek and the swampy flat of the clearing to a spot against a rock where we would camp, over-looked by the towering ridges on both sides and from down the valley where we had come. The only sight of lesser altitude was to the west further into the recess of Rum Gully, but in fact that was the same once the next moraine was climbed and the head of the valley entered.

We decided to camp in a spot where the ground was still quite swampy, although not as much so, as the only alternative some yards away. As this spot gave us the added protection of a large rock that we could lean out of the tent and cook under, we stuck with it, and a good spot it turned out to be.

First we collected twenty or so roundish rocks about eight to twelve inches in diameter and set them out as a platform over which we set up the tent. This would give us elevation above the swamp; although left like that would make a very uncomfortable bed. Then we set to work to cut sheets of moss off the trunks of trees nearby and lay them out in the tent until it was literally full to the ridge. John squeezed in and flattened the moss as much as he could and then Rodger joined him bouncing up and down to flatten the mass and when the level was low enough I joined in and we ended up with the rocks so covered that we couldn't feel them at all and had a soft base. We then spread a sheet of black polythene over the moss and we were set. Over the next few days that we hunted the gully that bed became the most comfortable that I have ever known in the hills.

In the late evening we had decided, probably wrongly, to have a quick look up over the nearby moraine, which was bush covered, to gain a look into the head basin of Rum Gully as a preparation for the next day. Being the youngest, I was relegated to the back of the single file line that we made as we negotiated the tall crown fern under the trees which in their moss-draped lower branches presented a wonderland to walk through. Steadily climbing on a gentle pitch I was all eyes, used to the knack of walking with a minimum of looking at my feet and the ground ahead.

The ability to memorize several paces ahead as you walk through the bush is a valuable asset releasing your eyes for the more important task of hunting for that ear, tail or leg of an animal that indicates the presence of your quarry. John and Rodger obviously weren't doing as well as I in that department – though to be fair they hadn't had the last few years of intense hunting as I had had - as they missed seeing the back of a deer protruding over the crown fern directly in front of them, one that they would spook in moments if they didn't look up.

For the second time that day I had to hiss a warning at a calculated volume to alert them of a deer in front of them without disturbing the deer. It worked, and we all ducked down at John's urgent bidding. He called me forward to take the shot as I had seen it first, and as soon as it lifted its head, confirming it was a female, the seven by fifty seven downed it. My first non-red deer, a wapiti cow. Not something that a lot of hunters would see as the ideal of success, but it had to be taken into account that we were here on a culling trip to knock the numbers down for the betterment of the herd, or so we were told and I as a nineteen year old believed.

The shot echoed alarmingly around the cliffs that rose to the dimming skyline steeply above. How many deer did we lose the next day because of that shot, I wondered. John showed Rodger and me how to do all the measurements and weighings for research reasons on the dead deer and we soon returned to our camp with meat from the young cow and high hopes for the next day.

The frail triangle that the temporary shelter of the tiny tent made, with its out of place artificial colouring against the massive bulwarks of the eternal mountains behind commented allegorically on the vulnerability of man in the perspective of the unimaginable grandeur of entire creation. I went to bed that night with feelings that I am sure many a Fiordland hunter has had in that wonderful country that seems to carry the very awe of God in its heart-bursting beauty.

This was the tent, now sagging in a coating of dew, that I woke up in before the others. I was waiting for the light to seriously announce its arrival with the smudgy faintness of gray sneaking into the blackness of the night, and my first real day of hunting in Fiordland to start. I could tell that it was another beautifully fine February day as the smell of the dew and the coolness of the air drifted about but was unable to enter the snugness that I was feeling deep in my sleepingbag and soul.

The steady breathing and stillness of the other two in the tent slowly merged into a preawake restlessness as my being awake altered the rhythms that had kept going all night, and before long arms were being pushed into sleeves from sitting bodies still ensconced in feather fluffed bags to the hips. The smallness of a two to three man pup tent with three men in it getting dressed for a day on the hill makes a liar of the manufacturer's claims. It was definitely a two man tent, full stop. However the small primuses were soon machinegunning away as porridge was being burnt to the bottom of aluminium billies steadily resisted by Rodger. We emerged into the stillness of a cool dew laden valley and the promise of a blue sky to each radiate away some yards and backs all turned to each other, water some tree trunk or weed in silence.

The day was a beaut and the initial hurdle of getting out of warm and cozy bedding to don cold woolen shirts and shorts, which seemed very inadequate, was over. The porridge adjusted our body temperatures and filled our bellies with warmth and we were feeling the joy of being here and being fit and able to put in

One Day in Fiordland

a good day. "Lets be up and at it," our bodies said in unison and day packs were hurriedly assembled, rifles magazines were loaded after the barrels were given their obligatory dry pull through and boots and puttees were tightened around eager feet and calves.

Off we went across the flat of the swampy clearing, making tracks where our boots cleaned the dew off the long grass. Our first task was to climb through the bush over the first moraine where we had reconnoitered briefly the evening before, and soon we were all clambering onto a rock, that fitted only one of us, to catch our first sight of the valley head. Clouds of mosquitoes descended on us and bottles of insect repellent were suddenly needed and before we could even look around us the necessity of wiping the oily mixture all over our exposed skin took precedence. Then our eyes lifted to the surrounding expansive scene.

Some distance from us we could see the open grassy flat ever so slightly concaved that formed a lake in the center of the valley when the never far away rains fell and filled it. It was dry now and looked as if it would be good for a couple of football fields. Binoculars were to eyes and we spent some time glassing all the slopes that we could see from there. A fully mature wapiti cow was sighted way high on a tongue of grass that was crammed between two horrendously steep spurs of the south face of the valley. She looked as if she had access to the tops above her and we discussed if it would be possible to climb up there and get her. Finally John decided to go closer and have a look and Rodger and I would go on into the head basin.

Crossing the grass and moss bed of the dry lake and reaching the far end we decided to take one side of the valley each and stalk up through the bush to the open slopes under the cliffs where we would then meet up again. Taking the left side of the basin I was soon stalking through the ever present crown fern under the moss drapes of the trees. I thought the rain here surely

At Home in the Hills

must know how to fall to cause the depth and thickness of the moss that covered everything. It was a magnificent place to hunt through. So easy to be quiet.

Poking my nose out of a clearing I was confronted by the indignant frown of a huge wapiti cow above me at the far end of a clearing fifteen yards away. The way she held her head was certainly different than the way that a red does - something about the angle of the neck where it leaves the brisket. A slight difference in the proportions of face to ears to nose revealed a greater sense of intelligence I think.

Again a shot echoed in the valley and my partners were informed of what I was up to. She was a huge animal to me. I remember that the measurement from the tail tip along the spine, up the neck, over between the ears and on to the upper lip was ninety two inches. I also had to measure a front lower leg, weigh a kidney with and without the fat, and take the left jawbone. All this hurriedly but accurately recorded I stuffed the measuring gear in my pack and moved on as quickly as possible. I was aware that the shot would disturb other deer in the vicinity and more importantly that the other two guys were nearby and may get my share of them if I dropped behind. I needn't have been concerned.

Reaching the open slopes which rose up to where the cliffs encircled almost the whole valley all the way to Wapiti River, now way below and behind us, my eyes were instantly scanning left and right over all the likely country above. Rodger was not in sight and in fact didn't arrive for some time. John had given up on the cow on the high grass tongue and was somewhere in the bush behind me too probably making his way up to where I was as well. At the head of the valley is the only real exit out onto the tops for its whole length and its aperture only measures about twelve feet in width. That exit was only about a thousand feet or so above me now and I was here alone. Time to have a breather while I waited for the others to come up. I heard a distant branch snap in the bush below followed by an appropriate exclamation, and from that could pinpoint Rodger's path and calculate his arrival time. Quite a while yet.

Suddenly my eye caught a movement way up by the cliffs. Two cows making their way along where there was obviously a track under the cliffs from the south towards the only exit to the northwest of me. They paused, momentarily before continuing, looking back to a point well south of me and so I reasoned that John was making his way along there and that they either scented or heard him and were getting out of his way as fast as their mothers had taught them to. The nearest point their path would come to me would be about four hundred yards away and they would be there in about five minutes time. Too long a shot for me, especially seeing that they were moving steadily and probably would not stop.

Directly up above me and about two hundred yards away on the slope was a huge block of rock forming a flat terrace of some area, raised up from the slope about twenty feet high, and I immediately moved off fast for it. The deer went out of sight behind it as I approached underneath its base and I was pushing it and puffing hard, hoping to get there before they had gone past. Cresting the top they were right on the closest point they would get to me and trotted happily on, not having sighted me. That pace is a real ground covering one for a deer and it seems to be an extra efficient one for wapiti. They were not going to give me any time to stop puffing.

Quickly finding a suitable mound to lie behind and support my rifle on I dropped my pack and flopped into position wriggling to get as well situated as possible. Since early days I had learned to always get as good a rest as possible for my rifle so that I could ensure the greatest possibility of a good shot first time. Using bows and arrows and a single shot twenty two as my first rifle taught me this.

At a later time I was shooting with a guy who was using a semi automatic twenty two when we came across two rabbits racing across a dip in the ridge we were on. He opened up using up ten shots before his rabbit disappeared into the cover of the tea tree on the fence line. I had to take my time with the single shot knowing I only had one stab at it and swinging the rifle as I had learned to do while working for the Rabbit Board I passed the sight over the rabbit and advanced it just in front, before letting the only shot I had go. It was very satisfying to see the rabbit cartwheeling to a halt with the bullet having passed through its vital organs. One sure shot is always best. That doesn't mean that you will always hit what you are aiming at just because you took a bit more time or had a better rest, but it does mean that your kills will usually be cleaner and your average kills per shot will look more impressive.

The deer were still at least two hundred and fifty yards away and so the shots would be difficult for me. I am sure that a better shooter would not have had to use the shots that I did. One shot missed and the deer merely sped up their brisk pace. There was a steep spur coming down off the cliff that if they rounded would take them out of sight and give them free access to the exit from Rum Gully over to the tops above the Edith River beyond. The second shot missed. I wasn't sure how much lead to give a trotting deer with a seven by fifty seven at any range so was experimenting as I was firing these shots. The third shot gut shot the smaller of the two and it stopped and slowly lay down on a small ridge just at their disappearing point.

From here the other cow had to travel about thirty yards directly away from me before rounding the spur out of sight and

I knew that I had her as she presented a smaller but perspectively still shot. She dropped over the edge of a small slope to roll to the bottom stone dead. The gut shot one lay still with head raised watching me as I made my way up to her. Rodger was now in sight puffing his way up to me and John could be seen approaching some hundreds of yards to the south. Neither had seen the deer but had a lot to say about the fusillade they said that I had used. Five shots it had taken.

When I used to use a triple two while culling a year or so before this, as I have previously said, I had got into the habit of reloading quickly after a shot. One evening in the Pourangaki I had been returning to the hut down through the clearings behind the helipad when I had spooked a hind and let fly three shots in quick succession at her as she ran through the ferns and leaped over fallen logs etc.

The guys came out and whistled and yelled cheek at me from the hut a long way below where they had been fixing tea. When I stepped out of the darkness with a slinky skin from that hind the nickname "Machinegun Morrie" became the main topic of the evening's banter. 'Get enough lead in the air and you're bound to hit something' is the kind of theory that balances the cautious theorizing that I propagated above. There is a time for every season. A time to shoot fast and a time to shoot slow.

While still about a hundred yards from the wounded cow, a rattle from a rock slide to the north turned my head to see a big ten point wapiti bull trotting down towards me. It could see the wounded deer and me and was a little confused as to why the deer was seemingly at ease with me so near and was coming to investigate. I took several photos of him with my three hundred millimeter lens before he finally spooked at the arriving presence's of my two hunting mates and left at a high rate of knots. We watched him until he entered the bush way below towards the dry lake.

After doing the honors on the deer with my knife, all of us performing the measurements needed, we carried on to the gap in the cliffs above to the Edith tops.

We stepped over the top and immediately ducked. There was a strong wind pouring up the face of the Edith slopes and with watering eyes we peered out over the Tasman Sea, bright with the glare of the afternoon sun on it. Several beautiful emerald green native mountain parrots - Keas - were playing in the wind as it swept up the slope and we crouched behind rocks poking our cameras at them hoping to get close shots of them. John got a great shot of one of them that I saw some months later. They would open their wings up while way below us and the wind would catch them and hurl them up the slope to a point way above us. Then they would close their wings nearly all the way leaving only just enough to keep control and dive back down with a hissing and whistling of feathers till they were way below us again only to open them once more and catch the wind again and whoosh up above us, repeating the process again and again. It was great fun watching them play like children.

Then we noticed a deer feed its way out of a hidden gully about two hundred yards away around the sharp slope from us to the north. The one became two. A young twelve point bull joined them out of a crevice, and then more, and there were finally five. Three young bulls and two cows. Then a bark reached us from above on the ridge that climbed up to a peak forming a part of backing of the Rum Gully cliffs. After searching for a few moments we spotted a six point bull up there watching us that had become alarmed, enough to stand up and blurt out his concern to the others below.

John and Rodger followed the five around the slope out of sight where they had moved at the barking and I stayed behind. I had already shot three and they hadn't got any so far. Two shots rung out and a little later they came back. John's two seventy had done the trick on both of the cows.

While relaxing there sucking some chocolate we noticed two more bulls lying on a ridge to the south of us enjoying the afternoon sun. They were about six hundred yards away at least and due to the strong wind had not been alarmed. Through the binoculars we could see that they sported ten point and fourteen point heads respectively. We watched them for a long time and they could see us as well but didn't seem worried. Finally though, they rose and trotted off around their ridge away to the south along the bulldozed track that was very deep and well used there.

A hanging valley about a thousand feet below us in the Edith side had a nice green clearing in it surrounded by a flat bush covered area. It was steeply below us and inaccessible from where we were. While we sat there with the bulls lying away to the south of us I was impressed with the view from that spot. Range after range of steep and jagged peaks stretched forever away to the north as far as the eye could see. Valleys were hidden from view by them showing only the tantalizing promise of their secrets through the saddles and dips on their ridge lines and I felt their drawing power as never before.

I have always been one to wonder what was around the next bend in a river or over the next ridge, but the fascination of that spot surpassed all such feelings I had had like that before. I wanted to simply roam off northwards and explore all those distant horizons, unheeding of the obvious dangers. The fact that I had no overnight gear was the only thing that battled with the notion, and I felt equally caught between the necessity of returning to the tent so far away below us by nightfall and the desire to simply go into those magical mountains that my eyes were devouring and my heart was yearning for spread at my feet.

At Home in the Hills

It was a very dissatisfying thing to turn my boots back through the gap in the cliffs of Rum Gully an hour or so later.

Swinging my binoculars back over the flat in the hanging valley way below in the Edith again, I noticed that there was a yearling who had come out from the bush surrounding it. As I watched it I realized that it was playing chase with a paradise duck that was reluctantly a part of the game. We all watched and were highly amused as the young deer leapt and frolicked as a kitten does toying with a ball of wool. It was a real entertainment for a time until another deer wandered into view in the clearing, and then another and another and another. Finally in that clearing we were able to see fourteen deer that had risen from their sleeping places as the afternoon had begun to slip into early evening. But we reluctantly realized that we had a long way to go and that time was in fact short. The wind was getting a bite to it and we were huddling deeper and deeper into our coats.

We had been perched here on this high eirie in the sky taking in the wonder of the place too long. With stretching of stiffening legs we rose and donned packs again, feeling the cool wind sneak into the gaps between our clothes and skin where we had been tightly wrapped up, keeping that very air out. It sneaks up the bottom of your shorts and down your neck where you feel most vulnerable, making you suck in and hold your breath and move quickly to get the blood circulating again.

The long trip down to the bush line and then on to the lake bed was a sad one, interrupted only with the spooking of another bull that flowed over a log jammed gut covered with greasy mosses as if it flew. My thoughts were on the mountains that had been etched into my mind far above as they stacked all over each other, jumbling and cramming together as I had seen them, and can see them still some twenty eight years later. I have not as yet been able to return. Still I'm not old yet.

One Day in Fiordland

I was my normal quiet self of those days as we plodded back to the tent arriving with reluctance just after dark. My heart was still up on the ridge. Lying in my sleeping bag that night after a warm meal and several hot brews, it took some time to get to sleep. I never loved being in the mountains more than I did that night and I didn't want the day to end. However there are some things that you can't do anything about, and before long I was as deeply asleep as the others.

The remaining days of the trip held many aspects that were very memorable. There were more deer for me to shoot and more valleys and hidden lakes to find and explore. There was a torrential night of rain to marvel at and John, Rodger and I caught a wapiti fawn, and all of us enjoyed its inquisitive company about the hut. We watched two native flightless Wekas race around Hankinson Hut and I blew the fire out one night by throwing an ammunition box in the fire that I had mistakenly thought was empty. It had had one more bullet in it that went off with a bang, silencing all conversation and extinguishing the fire that had taken some time to light due to the wet wood.

We had heard the mosquitoes in the night querying each other over whether to eat us as we lay, or to take us outside and eat us there, finally deciding to eat us inside the hut or the big ones would take us off them outside. It was a trip full of experiences, but on that day I had seen thirty three deer and some of the most magnificent country ever. It had been a great day in Fiordland

CHAPTER ELEVEN
A Few More Odd Deer

NEAR MISSES

Miro valley was really my learning ground as a young hunter, and from it the techniques of life in the hills were slowly gained and a good foundation laid for me. It is thick secondary-growth bush mostly and can be difficult to get through in many places. The streams that intertwine in a maze of directions over the flatter, areas where you can't see the surrounding peaks and that I haven't completely explored even yet, taught me more about direction finding than I have learned anywhere else. There are areas of great steepness with deep gorges, and waterfalls up to two hundred feet in height creating impassable barriers in places, and occasionally, too occasionally, there are some easy places. When you see a deer in that bush it can only be close.

One day while pushing through a particularly thick scrubby piece high on the windward face of a ridge, where the trees are stunted and the foliage thickest, I nearly walked right into a hind. Pushing aside a wiry branch amongst a thousand similar, there in front of me was the shocked and wide eyed face of a mature bony hind looking over her shoulder at me. Her rump was in easy kicking distance, but I was so surprised, as she was, that I didn't even think, "load up" before she leapt away. One bound and she was out of sight, crashing away through the wiry twigs and branches of the wind-blasted, stubby trees. She must have been twenty or thirty feet away before I regained my wits and finally pushed the bolt down on the Sako 243, which had become an extension of my arm over those years, and began peering through the branches looking for a shot. I was only miles too slow and she was one hind that didn't do the embarrassing trip for a deer of being carried the five hours over the distant ridge on my back for sale at Rongotea.

I got such a fright once when a hind barked from a point very near me, where I hadn't seen her, that I dropped my rifle. Before I could pick it up she was gone around the side of the bush face on the Mokai Range and I never saw her again. Frustrating that, especially when you need the tail or carcass to earn your keep.

Two Stags

Another time I saw a fern flicking and jerking from its position behind the turned up, clay clogged roots of a large tree that had been pushed over by Rua Mudgeway's bulldozer as he had been logging in the area and making the muddy track that I was trying to move quietly up. I had found that Rua's presence in the area, pushing over miles of trees to make access tracks to the few large Rimus that raised their weeping tops out of the lower bush, was a real help to me as a meat hunter. The deer would frequent the track, feeding on the freshly accessible leaves from the pushed down trees. I got a few deer because of the D4E that he owned.

Seeing the fern flicking there I was sure that only a deer could be moving it like that. There had been the unsettling cackling and squawking of black birds in the stillness of the evening as I had made my way dodging around the worst of the mud of the recently opened up track edging further and further through the shadows toward the track's end. But it wasn't a blackbird moving that fern. The fallen trees had brought a lot of foliage into reach of deer, and the track was strewn with fresh deer foot marks coming and going along its length.

Creeping in my lace-up gumboots along the muddy edge of the logging track, in the mid-winter bush, I slowly closed on the jerking frond watching its continued movement confirm the animal's unalarmed presence. Finally, I peered over the dirt clogged roots of the upturned tree with tense caution. There, six feet from me were the ears of a deer. I didn't raise my head any further, as at this level it still wasn't able to see me. It hadn't heard or smelt me either, so quietly lowering the bolt of the 243 and cautiously lifting it over my head at arm's length, I pointed it just lower than the ears which then froze in frightened stillness. I could only imagine the deer's eyes that must have rolled up without any movement of the head assessing this apparition, which being so close surely couldn't be what it appeared to be.

I fired probably a split second before the message from the stag's eyes got to its brain and was translated to the muscles to end in stampede. He fell right there. That is the closest that I have ever stalked up to a deer without it knowing that I was there. I shot another stag as close as that which I mention further on in this chapter, but that one came to me as I roared to it, and so it was in the season when stags don't have their wits about them as they do in the middle of winter.

One of his antlers was deformed and lay alongside his face ending in a big knob just below his jaw. The other was normal but didn't have the mass of the malformed one. It didn't matter to me at the time as he was headed for the Consolidated Traders' freezer at Rongotea minus his head anyway. Lashing his floppy

At Home in the Hills

gutted carcass to the pack frame that I was carrying just for that purpose, I began to make my way down the track making no real effort to avoid the sucking of my boots in the sticky mud now. The pack straps cut into my shoulders in their familiar way and I would shift their position continuously as I moved to hold off the necessity of a rest. I usually left a deer where it lay for a day so that the body was stiff before carrying it out, as it didn't wobble about so much then. As this one was only half an hour from the grass of the farmland and forty minutes from my van, I decided to carry it, uncomfortable as it was, straight away.

Jim Warren and the author (left) at Ruahine Corner Hut (1969).

Twenty minutes later, while I was still carrying him down the track to my car, I heard a twig snap and turned to see another stag feeding beside the track about twenty yards away. He was a beauty and the sight of him is still in my mind. Such a well proportioned, fit and sleek animal with classic coloring. He was reaching high, twisting and tensing his neck to pull the twigs off an erect branch of a small tree that had been downed as the track was put through, and his black antlers were laying back over his spine in a magnificent pose. His back legs were half bent trying to lift his front legs off the ground to get that last bit of advantage, with the elusive leaves almost out of reach. He looked so strong, with the promise of great speed and agility hovering about every part of his body. A wild stag. Aren't they something else?

It was difficult to fit the rifle to my shoulder as the dead weight of the deer on my back was holding me at an awkward angle, and the pack straps over my shoulder were right where I wanted the rifle to hug into me. However, the urgency of the moment, the closeness of the stag, and the familiarity of my rifle overcame any disadvantages and his antlers found a place on the Punga Hut. The money that I got for the two also found a place, but did not last as long as the antlers and the memory did.

I have heard meat hunters talked of in derogatory terms over the years, and I suppose that there are some who have deserved it. I've certainly met some that did. But there are, or should I say were, some that were in the meat hunting game of the seventies that weren't in it for the money, although they had to get enough deer to pay their bills. They were in it for the love of hunting. They were in it for the love of the bush and the life that they found there. Most of the time I was broke when meat hunting. I found others that hunted hard so as to make their load but I wasn't one of them. Some of them devised ways using horses, planes, even wheelbarrows, and, finally, helicopters to get more deer out of the bush more efficiently so as to make more dollars. I just loved the hunting and the life, and Miro Valley was the training ground for me. Now my boots have taken me over much of the North Island back country and that valley is one that I don't get to much. But it is a special place in my book.

The Magic Two Four Three

One night a young friend and I went to the Punga Hut for two days hunting and got there not long before dark on a Friday evening. I was feeling a bit restless and so decided to go for a quick look downstream to see of I could catch a deer out on the tiny side streams of the main creek, or in one of the clearings that I knew of. My young friend was a little tired from the trip in and didn't want to impede me, as it would be necessary for me to travel quickly due to the dwindling light. I was living off the deer that I shot at the time and so needed a cash flow to cover food and petrol for my Vanguard van that got me to the hills and back, and to the odd dance in town. It was much more suited for the former and was looked at with some disdain by others that traveled in it, from time to time, to or from the dances. Those Vanguard vans had the same motor in them that the old Ferguson tractors had, and sometimes that one had to prove its heritage and kinship on the last lengths of farm track that it took me to. It soon started to look like a Ferguson tractor. Yes, I guess I did too.

Not far from the hut, I caught a sight of some clearings about eight hundred feet above me to the east on what we called the back ridge, and turning my scope to it, I spotted a hind way up there feeding in the sheltered lee of a projecting knob. There wasn't much light left and the decision to go after it, although motivated a little by money, was overshadowed by the oncoming dark. I decided to have a go, knowing that the dark would probably get me, but I started moving fast and was soon running up the hill through the bush. It is wonderful to be so fit. I know that I will never be like that again. The memory of that run is still so vivid to me. The ground fairly threw me upward and my legs seemed to be able to push me into the air as if they were assisted by a series of trampolines. It was exhilarating. I gained the ridge top, took a couple of deep breaths and was not puffing anymore.

A Few More Odd Deer

The deer carrying I'd done in the last months over rough country and through thick bush, sometimes for five and six hours and more, had done a good job on my legs. All the sweat and strain of doing a hard job paid the dividend that I reaped in times like that evening.

While quickly traversing a saddle on the main ridge top I spooked a stag which reappeared two hundred yards further along. It was high tailing it uphill and directly away from me through a clearing on a steep knob, with my obviously putrid stench still in his nose. The only thing that I came close to running away from with that degree of conviction was my Mum carrying the castor oil bottle and a tablespoon. Leading the crosshair two feet above the climbing profile of the stag's nose I let the shot fly and he slammed into the ground with a broken spine. Good old Sako two four three.

Getting to him as fast as possible I quickly gutted him, and then wondered if the hind that enticed me up to this ridge was still there on the other side of the knob where I had first sighted her. As it was only about one hundred yards from where the stag fell I doubted it due to the reverberating echo that the shot had made. However, there she was, feeding undisturbed. I am sold on the 243 for a deer calibre. It shoots flat, recoils little, and doesn't make as much noise as some of the larger cannons. I gutted the hind out too in the last vestige of light that this day would give me, leaving them to be picked up tomorrow, and headed back to the hut and my young friend.

It was soon so dark that I had to touch my eyes to see if they were open on my trip back in the bush, and it took a long time. I never carried a torch in those days. I don't know why. It just didn't occur to me. I climbed down on the ridge as far as I could before dropping into a small creek. From there I edged over the slippery waterfalls and fallen trees covered with moss by feel, and

At Home in the Hills

through the jungle-like bush carefully protecting my eyes, one tested step at a time. It was funny how over the years the fear that I had first felt being in the bush after dark had so completely gone. I enjoyed it now. Traveling in the bush after dark without a light, I think that you develop an affinity, through physical touch and sixth sense feel, that doesn't happen otherwise. I guess that it's a little like developing the senses as a blind person does and getting a different perspective of the world from most people. It is also a good way to get lost.

When I arrived back at the hut my young mate, Tony, was in a slightly worried state. He had stayed in the hut once it had gotten dark, except for one short trip outside and a very fast retreat back into it. Somehow the corner of the hut had cast a weird shadow which had caught him by surprise, pumping his blood pressure up, and he probably lost the expectation of living into his eighties there and then. At least ten years off his life he reckoned.

When he had more colour back in his face I began rummaging around in the hut preparing for the night. He made us both a brew and mistakenly put salt into his instead of sugar. He nearly vomited his first sip out onto the floor. When salt is a bit moist from sitting in a plastic bag in a bush hut for too long it sticks together a bit and can look like the heavier crystals of sugar.

I'd recently read a book that had a story in it about a mechanic working with a new apprentice. The new apprentice under the car had accidentally grabbed the very hot exhaust pipe and yelled appropriately. The mechanic, using all the authority of his seniority, urgently told him to instantly grab it again and that would seal the burn and stop the pain. The poor apprentice did so and had the next few weeks off work with serious burns. I think that the mechanic should have got some time off too, but without pay.

Inspired by this though, I quietly told my young 'apprentice' that the way to fix the tea was to put four teaspoons of sugar into it. The first two would counteract the salt and the next two would sweeten it. He did vomit the first sip of that out onto the floor.

As judgment, I guess, when I returned to the two deer at daylight the next day, they were flyblown beyond saleable condition. Although I had pulled them under a bush and covered them with layers of long grass and flat lying branches, the interminable flys had still gotten through. Usually layers of fronds covering a deer in a cool place can preserve the deer in very fresh condition. The buyers at Rongotea Consolidated Traders took some fairly dirty deer from me at times, but I knew that they wouldn't take those ones.

Waikatore Stag

The sweeping view from Potae in the Northern Ruahines is a three sixty degree one because of the steepness of the pointed peak. Seated on the big rock at its southern extremity, I was enjoying being there that April morning as the sun climbed higher and higher into a clear blue sky. Ohutu Ridge stands broadly across the western horizon flanked by the peaks of the Ruapehu, Ngaruahoe and Tongariro volcano's and the Kaimanawa Ranges behind. These give way to the Otupae Range and distant Kaweka Ranges to the north which dip to the skyline of the Ikawatea watershed and the Main range of the Ruahines out towards No Mans Hut and its vast surrounding mountain area. From there the view marches on down the spine of the old woman, Ruahine, to the south, even revealing the distant faint blue peaks above the Oroua River that I could make out that day over the progressively closer Pourangaki, Kawhatau, Waikamaka, Maropea and Mangatera river systems, the last of which struggled up to meet me at my feet. To the southwest, finishing the panorama, stands the high point of Rongotea at the head of the Mokai Patea Range, who'se golden tussock stretches and rolls westward to successfully dive, after a false attempt at the Mokai saddle, into where the Maropea and Rangitikei Rivers fork. This is also where the nearby bulk of Ohutu Ridge climbs out northwards to finish the circle.

My good hunting mate, Dennys Smith, had left that morning with Jim Warren for Makirikiri Hut and the Otupae Range to retrieve a twelve point head from there that Jim had shot a few weeks before. They would be gone two days so I decided to go down to the Waikatore Tent camp overnight for a bit of a hunt and a looksee.

Reluctantly, I dropped down off the peak a few yards to where the track to Waikatore Stream and the permanent tentcamp established there branches off westward from the more used one that continues on to Colenso hut and the middle reaches of the Mangatera river. I was soon swinging along through the beautiful bush, rising and falling over the rolling ridge top where the track meanders. It was a beautiful day and the cool of the bush was hinting at the coming of winter. There was a real sense, in all the bush's subtle statements, of closing down for the cold that would cover the land for some months ahead, before the returning sun turned the forces of nature about again so that new growth would announce spring later in October. The ground was cold and, when stopping for any length of time, that cold quickly transferred to toes, even inside boots, and began to numb them. The foliage that had been fresh and new only a few months ago now everywhere showed oldness and weathering. The beautiful day didn't have the heat of summer, but, though conveying an enjoyable and clear warmth it carried a threat of dangerous coolness in its breath. It was just the kind of weather that rutting stags react to noisily.

After a couple of hours of easy strolling along alone, realizing that I had no one to check in with and no time table to keep, I sat down for a swig of my water bottle and a bit of a bar of chocolate. The bush was quiet and I began to think that maybe there was no roaring going on down here. Looking out through the bush towards the distant Black Hill, I surmised that there must be a bit of a cliff nearby on that side of the ridge as the trees finished abruptly in that direction, about fifty yards away. I picked up my Sako 243 and strolled over to have a look, munching my chocolate bar.

The cliff dropped about fifty feet and then the ground sloped away in a narrow old slip that was covered with grass, ragwort and thistles, bounded on both sides with the ever present beech forest. As I could see down over hundreds of acres of bush, and the day was so still, I lifted the cow's horn from around my neck and let out a long, low, and loud moan hoping that it could be heard for some way. Instantly, from a creek about three hundred yards away, an answer came back to me in an urgent bellow from an obviously young stag. It was all on. He was really keen and I felt, rightly, that he had immediately begun to come to me.

While continuing to roar back and forth to each other, I quickly scouted along the cliff top to find a way down below it into the bush so that I would be able to get close to him. A suitable gap in the cliff belt appeared and I was soon on the clearing and dropping down, looking for a deer trail that would sidle to my left to take me above the stag and forcing his line of approach to me to be from below. The roaring that was coming from him left me no feelings of anxiety that you can often have with a stag that they may lose interest or simply stop roaring and you may lose them. This boy was looking for trouble.

I soon found what I was looking for and was making my way along a good trail out of the clearing, sidling to the left in nicely open bush around the spur towards a shallow and wide valley that opened up down from the cliffs to the distant valley below.

At Home in the Hills

The tall beeches were fairly well spaced and visibility was up to a hundred yards through the trunks, made even better from a hunting perspective by the fact that the undergrowth was mostly of low ferns no more than two feet high, these being interspersed with generous gaps of bare earth. Moving little, and roaring much to my eager quarry whose voice was getting clearer and clearer, I finally peered into the wide valley and there he was.

From about eighty yards away I watched him picking his way right up the middle of the valley in a quick stride that said he was on an important mission. I watched his eyes roll and shift from side to side, wide open, showing the whites out of proportion in his intensity of purpose as he climbed. He had no trophy head but he was a large bodied and healthy animal with black stained legs and under body of a mature, rutting stag. There was a three foot diameter trunk of a fallen tree lying lengthwise down the easy sloped ridge top, and I picked it to crouch behind as the stag stalked up the valley parallel to me.

When he reached the same contour as me, yet fifty yards away in the valley as I was on the ridge, fearing he may walk past I poked a fully loaded and cocked rifle over the log and let out a muffled roar from my hiding place. With an angry growl he swung around in my direction and, wild eyes searching the hillside, began striding along the continuation of the deer trail that I was on which led up to, and over, the log that I was behind. Suddenly the situation became interesting. I hadn't even been sure that I would shoot this stag. I had come down off the cliffs with the thought of a little bit of fun. Suddenly the stag was making up my mind for me.

The gap was closing fast and my eyes were fixed on him, I could see him picking his foot falls as he was nearly breaking into a trot towards me. Thirty feet, twenty feet and he still hadn't seen me. At ten feet I could see that he was going to jump the

A Few More Odd Deer

log and wouldn't see me probably until he landed on me. I wasn't keen on that idea, so my finger tightened on the trigger and the shot caught him in the brisket as he hunched his back legs his front legs just leaving the ground. The shot didn't stop the coiled muscles of his back legs, releasing but it did stop them propelling his weight forwards just enough, and he went straight upwards, about five feet off the ground, and landed on his back right where he had jumped from - quite dead.

I'm sure that it wasn't the hundred and ten grains of 243 that had knocked him back and stopped him from landing on me but was, in fact, his last second reaction to escape the totally unexpected explosion under his nose. I wondered later if I should have let him jump on me as that would have been an even more unusual story to tell. However, I think that it is unusual enough and could be unbelievable even as it stands for some.

When you have spent a lot of time in the bush hunting you accumulate a lot of memories. Most of the deer that you shoot and things that you see are not above the ordinary, yet you can't miss having the unusual happen from time to time. All hunters have these strange occurrences, and, although I have heard tales that even I can't believe, I usually give the benefit of the doubt to the storyteller as truth is often stranger than fiction. And what harm is done if you have believed a lie anyway. It is a virtue to trust and immoral to lie. If you mistakenly believe a lie you have at least shown a virtue. It is not you who should be ashamed, but the person that misled you.

Thinking of that stag later made me wonder what the roar is like for hinds. I guess we have guys like that in the human world too, but for the hinds the whole mating thing is crammed into only a few weeks of the year so the intensity of it all must be much more concentrated. These mad stags must be a handful for any hind.

At Home in the Hills

THINGS THAT FLY

It has always been a fascination of mine to watch things fly. I believe that this fascination is one of the contributing factors to my love of hunting. It is the flight of a bullet or an arrow, or a spear, of course, that has been the technology behind our life in the wilderness. From a young age it has been these things that have taken up a lot of my imaginings.

The first thing that I remember noting that flew was an aeroplane over Lower Hutt where I was born and lived, way back in the hazes of my memory when I learned to walk - a skill that has been the backbone of my life. More so than the average I think. I decided to be a pilot there and then. It never happened, but I have always loved to fly.

I was, thankfully, saved from a fate and destiny concocted from the city ways when my parents decided to move to the small town of Mangaweka where my father accepted a job as the town clerk, back in nineteen fifty five. We moved into a house backing on to the primary school where I began to be educated and which had, as former transient residents, the animals of a traveling circus. That circus used to return each year and was a firm part of the entertainment for us as a small and isolated community. It is not such an isolated life there now with the improvement of roads and vehicles etc. During the year before we moved there was a bountiful crop of hemlock growing in the yard where we later played as kids, but the circus folk didn't know what it was. That ignorance lead to the demise of one of their elephants. I don't know where they buried it. Quite a thing to bury and elephant.

Later working for the Rabbit Board in the Manawatu, I had to bury many cows, and even a horse once, minus the legs which I kept as meat for my dogs. They were given to me when they either broke a leg or died inexplicably. On a hot summer day in drought hardened ground you have your work cut out for you digging a hole big enough for a cow's torso. I'd hate to have to dig a hole for an elephant.

Since seeing my first aeroplane and being captured by the way that it moved in the air, I have loved flying. My first sight of Ruahine Corner was from the back seat of a light Cessna four seat aircraft, with a sugar bag of food supplies on my lap. My friend Dennys and I planned a February trip into the Mangaohane Plateau area, and I had shot a few deer to pay my half of the cost of an air drop. Neither of us had done an airdrop before, but how hard could it be? Dennys' boss had a pilot's license and, although he had never even heard of an airdrop being done before, he was willing to have a go. So, at six o'clock one Saturday morning, we headed out on to the runway of Milson Airport in Palmerston North.

Soon we were slowly climbing our way over Kimbolton township towards Rangiwahia enroute to the Northwest Ruahine block. As we covered the ground northwards, a thin belt of early morning gray cloud scudded over us, locking us underneath it. We were hoping that it would break up soon or rise in altitude so that we could proceed over the ranges to the magic Mangaohane area. However, it wasn't long before we could see that the cloud butted straight into the side of the Whanahuia and Hikurangi ranges, and further north from that lay so low over the farmland that we would never gain our objective underneath it either. We began to fear that we would not get to Ruahine Corner.

Suddenly my head hit the sack on my knees hard and, try as I might, I could not lift it off. Dennys was undergoing the same problem and we were pushing with all our strength to merely sit up again, but without success. Finally, our heads popped up on their own as the pilot, as suddenly as he had violently pulled back on the stick, pushed it forward. He had decided on the spur of the moment, with a wink at his mate in the front seat with him, to shoot upwards through the cloud and see what the view was like above it. Dennys and I had discovered multiple gravities. They got some mileage out of our greenness as they laughed for the next while.

Now we were above the cloud in brilliant sunshine, roaring along over a flat carpet of soft gray cloud that seemed to stretch to the horizon in all directions. The problem became how to get under it again over the Corner hut to drop our food supplies. We cruised along in the general direction hoping for a hole that we could slip back down through. It seemed to be an impossible prospect. I could see our dollars burning up as the engine sucked the gas that we were paying for through its system. We were probably going to arrive back at Milson with all of or food still on our laps.

Then we saw a hole in the cloud. Swerving over to it the pilot angled the wings sharply up so that my window was looking down the hole where I could see a jumble of bush covered ridges and valleys flash past in a second.

"Did you recognize it?" he said. I was the only one who had real knowledge of the area at the time and so it was my job to find out where we were.

"No," I replied, and we flew on looking for another hole. We, or should I say I, looked down several holes in the same fashion, trying to keep my weight from falling onto the seemingly flimsy door. It would have been all right if it had only been my weight but, with the added weight of the sugar bag full of tins and other assorted food items on my lap, and Dennys and his bag falling onto me too from the other side of the seat, I felt decidedly insecure.

Finally we flew over a particular hole and there below me was an unmistakable landmark in peaceful seclusion. The calm and beautiful waters of Lake Colenso, surrounded by cliffs and wide shingle river flats of the Mangatera looked demurely back at me.

"Yes, down there," I said to the pilot. There is a big valley there and we're not far from the Mangaohane." Suddenly all direction and perspective was wrenched from me as the plane swung tightly to the right and upwards, curving quickly. Then turning on its wing tip we dropped down into the hole, swooping out over the Mangatera valley under the cloud. I had no idea which way we were facing, and twisted quickly in all directions trying to find a horizon somewhere above, beside or below us, I didn't know which. I had lost up and down, as well as all other directions, in the confusion of a sideways somersault.

The frantic yelling of the pilot, who knew which way up was but had to make a decision about sideways very quickly, filled the small cabin of the plane and urgently motivated my frantic search for equilibrium. Suddenly the tussock of the Mangaohane Plateau dropped down into the window frame from where it had been hiding above the roof line, and I could see the Kaikawaka forest of the Waikatore Stream sloping back to us from up there. Leaning forward between the pilot and his friend, who weren't laughing now, I yelled, "Up there", pointing to a narrow slot of airspace between the gray ceiling of cloud and the high tussock plateau.

There was only about two hundred feet of flying room under the cloud around the tiny orange hut on the bush line, which, with a very serious expression, the pilot seemed to feel wasn't enough. We did wide circles looking for a place to drop the sacks where we would be able to find them a few days later. Deciding to aim for a particular spot, I tied my safety belt up a bit tighter and unlocked the door on my side. It was easy to open it for the first two inches but after that it took real effort. Finally it took both Dennys and I, using all our strength, to open it up enough, against the wind of our speed and the propeller, to squeeze the first bag out. I needn't have worried about doing up my seat belt so tight as there was no danger of falling out. It would have taken a very concerted effort to have squeezed anyone out of that door The belt so restricted my movement that I undid it for the next bag.

We had tied long strips of old curtain material to the sacks to make them easier to see as they fell, and also to ensure that they landed on the ends that we had put extra padding into. As each one dropped the pilot banked around so that we could watch out the window and note the places that they landed. It all worked out fine and we watched them hit the ground and bounce and bounce and bounce across the tussock until they came to rest quite well hidden from a ground-level observer.

Having completed our task, we swept away from the plateau shooting down over the Waikatore tent camp, out over the Rangitikei River and back to Palmerston North, getting back to our homes to find our families still in bed enjoying a Saturday morning sleep in. We had had an adventure already.

That afternoon we started the three day journey, up the Makaroro River to the Centre Makaroro Hut, from where, we climbed up onto Te Atuamahuru where we secured a nice roaring stag. Then we followed the Main Range over Tupari, dropped into the Ikawatea Stream, climbed up to the Potai track and wandered down to Ruahine Corner Hut. Then collecting the bags from where they had bounced to we found that there was not a single tin in them that was in its original shape. However only one was split and that was a tomato sauce can which had suffered little loss of its contents.

Planes are wonderful things and helicopters are too. As I've used up my time on planes I won't tell the story of the drunk pilot that picked us up from Lake Hankinson at first light one morning only to head straight back into an ugly belt of black cloud rolling over Fiordlands high peaks to retrieve other hunters from the seaward side of the range. He got them too. Maybe the drink helped him.

A Few More Odd Deer

But there are other kinds of things that fly that have grabbed me quite unlike aeroplanes. I have always been drawn to anything that makes an arc in the air as it goes.

Early on I became fascinated with the flight of a knife spinning about itself as it flew to a target. Probably another product of the Circus that used to come to town each year. I watched that man throw knives at balloons and place them around the still body of a woman, and I became absorbed with the flight of the knife. It wasn't long before I was throwing any knife I could get my hands on into shed walls, boards leaned up against a fences, or into trees. I learned how far away to stand from a target for different length knives if you wanted to stick it into the target after it completed one turn, or one and a half, or two turns. You had to hold it by the blade or the handle depending on how far away from your target you were.

I went through many knives over the years. Some broke at the joint of the handle and the blade. Several broke the tips off as they stuck into hardwood targets not quite straight. The weight of the handle moving off the line of the spin of the knife kept going when the point of the knife stopped in the hard wood and "ping," another ruined knife. It was a costly apprenticeship.

We had a large pepper tree about three feet in diameter in the back yard of a house in Linton that we lived in. It had an ideal trunk shape and softwood consistency that I found useful. However, over the years that we lived there, the tree slowly died, branch by branch, until it finally and completely snuffed it. My knives did it in. My first and only true victim of knife throwing.

As a small boy about eight, nine and ten years old living at Mangaweka we had often gone swimming and picnicking as a family to the Rangitikei river, by, what was then known as the Swing Bridge. An evening sport was to throw stones over the river. It was quite a long throw and I used to enjoy competing with the adult men at it. Watching the stones in flight encouraged me to throw them higher and further so that I could watch them for longer. My throwing arm got better and better. I was a thin and bony kid while I was growing up, so I was surprised later on when I attended the Palmerston Boys High School to find that I could throw both the shot put and the javelin as far as much bigger kids than I. Because the shot put had no fascination in its flight I let it go, but the javelin was another story. It really flew.

I broke the intermediate javelin record at high school when I was in the fourth form by eleven feet. A few minutes later another guy bettered my throw by another eleven feet, and, as I had used up my three attempts, his record held for the day. However I was able to attempt it again within the next seven days, and it took all of those to talk one of the teachers into giving up a precious ten minutes of his lunch break to come out to the field. On my second attempt I gained another nineteen feet on the new record. Suddenly there were teachers everywhere and, unfortunately, one of them erected a wind meter. The wind was going at one foot per second too much for my record to stand. I thought that it was a bit off, as the wind that I was throwing in was a head wind and would only have hindered my throw and not assisted it. Also the distance that I had exceeded the six day old record by could not have been accomplished by that small a wind excess, even if it had assisted my throw. I never quite forgave someone for that. I don't know who.

A consequence of that last throw, however, has lived with me from that day to this. I did something to my shoulder. I have never been able to throw as well as I used to, and I now get an extremely sharp pain there if I try. Watching things fly now took a different turn. They had to be propelled by another power.

For my twelfth birthday my parents bought me an archery bow and the first few of many arrows. Over the next four years until I was able to own a rifle I went through several grades of bow strength and many small animals heard the arrows buzz over their heads. I didn't miss all the time though.

Magpies, rabbits, eels, possums, hares and even pukekos all fell to my bow. Don't tell anyone about the pukekos. It was the beginning of learning to stalk animals and enjoy the hunt.

My friends and I played with a slug gun that I was allowed to own under my father's name before I was sixteen and we learned to shoot with it. It is a great way for a young person to learn to shoot, I think. The slugs are cheap and can be plugged away endlessly. They don't go far and therefore aren't so dangerous. They handle like a rifle and teach the hands and fingers the automatic responses necessary for carrying the weight for long periods, aiming fast, holding steady, and firing carefully. Most things that you shoot with a slug gun are small, so a person learns to shoot with attempted precision. We also used to throw tin cans into the air and shoot them at the top of the arc. That practice helped me to get a duck on the wing with a twenty two one dusk, and also to bring down more than a few running deer

The flight of balls also has been an interest of mine over the years. Tennis balls, table tennis balls and golf balls especially. Ones that you could guide with spin. It fascinated me how a twist of the wrist could lift a table tennis ball from inches of the floor and float it with a scooping shot several yards, almost hovering it over the net before it plopped onto the opponent's end. Or you could swing your arm from behind your back out to the side of your body collecting the ball as you go, creating a side spin that would curl the ball from a line outside of the edge of the table, lulling your opponent into thinking you had missed the table, but it would turn back again and skim off the corner of his end. I loved the flight of table tennis balls and managed to represent Manawatu once as a junior. They say that I could have done much more than that too but at eighteen deer hunting overtook all other interests.

At sixteen I bought my first rifle and from that time the flight of bullets has progressively taken most of my interest in that area. There has been so much said about this and I add the following with my tongue firmly in my cheek.

I will start by stating that my choice of a deer rifle for the conditions that I have hunted in is the two four three. It shoots flat and accurately and has sufficient power to drop a deer up to four hundred yards and more. I have used two, two four threes, two three nought threes, two seven by fifty sevens, a triple two, a three oh eight and seen twenty two, two fifties, two seventies, two, two threes, thirty oh sixes, six point fives by fifty fives and others in action, but my choice is the wonderful two four three. It just has it as far as I'm concerned. Even the numbers of its name fit together and sound good to me. If it were possible, my choice would be a Sako two four three action fitted to a Sako Vixen sized stock, with a twenty four inch barrel. I haven't seen a six point five oh eight in action yet, but I am very impressed with what I've heard about that caliber.

So, when it comes to this whole issue of what calibre should you use - which is best for your kind of hunting etc, I think that there are two issues that are dominantly important. One is your confidence in the rifle that you are using and the other is whether that rifle is capable of doing the job you are asking of it.

Your confidence in your rifle is the most important of the two. A person with a triple two, who is confident in his ability to hit his deer where he aims, will perform better than a person with a seven millimeter magnum who is not confident. Lack of confidence in a rifle will prompt a person to fire from a bad position, prematurely, and with insufficient concentration, passing off the poor result in blame of the rifle, or conditions, weather,

A Few More Odd Deer

or anything other than himself. If he is a young shooter then this kind of situation will talk him into believing that he is simply a poor shot. Confidence alone will produce a better shooter.

A person who is confident he can hit a particular target will hit it more often than a person that is not confident he can hit it. Confidence in a rifle will promote a shooter to take that little more time to get into good position, concentrate a little more fully and pick his spot of impact more precisely as he expects to hit where he aims and knows that any mistake is his fault alone. My mother said to me when I was just a young hunter of rabbits, that, using her rifle, any misses were my fault, for the rifle was spot on. To be a good shooter you have to have that attitude, and so confidence in your rifle is number one priority.

This affects calibre selection also as too much recoil will affect many peoples ability to fire well. I am like that and am unable to fire large calibres well as I anticipate the recoil and am apt to flinch. This affects my ability to shoot confidently and I shoot better with a smaller calibre.

Another thing that affects my ability to shoot confidently is probably a personal idiosyncrasy with no basis in reality. It is the noise that calibres make. A thirty oh six that was dropped suddenly on my shoulder on the only night that I ever spotlighted deer, deafened me for several moments and put me off that calibre for life. As I was carrying the light that night I ran after that deer, it was gut shot and had walked around the ridge out of sight. The guy with the thirty oh six kept alongside me as I hurtled along through the tussock in the dark after the deer. My mate, Dennys, was on my right with his three oh eight keeping pace too. I suddenly became aware of the thirty oh six guy not being with us anymore as we leaped over tussocks and raced through the night.

Topping a knob the light picked up the deer again only a hundred or so yards away and Dennys dropped it with a carefully placed shot. Soon after we arrived at the deer's lifeless carcass, the thirty oh six owner arrived a little worse for wear. He had run full speed into a hidden six foot deep hollow on the tussock ridge and hit the far side of it full length knocking the wind out of himself also burying his rifle barrel into the dirt clogging six inches of the bore. As my ear was still ringing I was not displeased. I don't like loud cannons.

Different calibres heard at distance are distinguishable because of their loudness. I believe that I have been able to shoot deer within short distances of each other because of the lesser noise that the smaller calibres make. I may be fooling myself here but that fooling of myself, if it is so, gives me more confidence in the two four three and lesser calibres and I value the confidence for its own sake. Over the last year or so I have been using a three oh eight and I don't like it. I bought it with the plan to put a different barrel on it but haven't been able to afford to do so yet. It does the job of felling deer very efficiently, but to me it fires too much lead, makes too much noise, kicks too hard, damages too much meat and usually puts two holes in the skin. I am not confident or efficient with it and find myself looking to see where the bullet hit when I walk up to the deer rather than know where it hit as I walk up.

The other issue of calibre selection is having a rifle that is capable of doing the job on the game that you are hunting. I have never hunted thar, or pigs purposely, and only rarely wapiti, so I am writing here about calibres for deer shooting only. I accept that to hunt those others, bigger calibres would probably be better.

I have shot several pigs, mostly by accidental encounter, and seen some shot over the years. One big boar was shot in the Tiritea valley by a culler named Darryl in the first week of my employment for the N.Z.F.S. He shot it four times in the head

A Few More Odd Deer

with an Anshutz triple two at very close range and each time, except the last one, it fell and got up again. I have shot several pigs very effectively with a twenty two putting the shot behind the ear but I wouldn't say that the twenty two is a good pig calibre. I don't think that the triple two or even the two four three would be really ideal for pigs either.

But back to calibres for shooting deer. The first thing to realize is that you only want one deer rifle. You don't want a rifle that is only good for bush hunting and another one for tussock shooting. The theory can sound right until the only deer that you see all day while hunting the bush is ten minutes from the hut as you are returning in the last rays of daylight. It happens to be almost out of sight walking around a bulge of a slip three hundred yards away across the valley. A stalk is impossible due to the dying light and you have just enough time for one shot before it's gone. The trouble is you only have in your hand your short barreled three oh eight with a one and a half power scope on it. It is shot in to a hundred yards with the one hundred and eighty grain blunt nose projectiles and you don't know how much fall they have over three hundred yards. It's now you wish that you had your tussock rifle with you. So you arrive back at the hut one bullet less and without a deer. I think that it is wiser to have one rifle that suits all situations. One thing that I am sure of is that if your rifle can hit accurately and kill a deer at three hundred yards it will hit and kill one at all ranges closer than that.

So the question is what calibres can kill a deer efficiently at what is long range for you? Some guys say, and I suppose have, shot deer at five hundred yards and further. I personally don't attempt those distances as I have no confidence for getting reliable kills there. For me four hundred yards is a very long shot and I have only shot two deer further than that. They both fell on the same day and, strangely enough, were downed with a triple two.

Most of the deer that we all shoot are less than fifty yard shots. A large number of the remainder are shot between fifty and one hundred and fifty yards. Some are shot between one hundred and fifty and three hundred yards and few are shot further away than that. However, you want to be able to get those few as any good rifle will be easily capable of hitting at four hundred yards if sighted in well. Then, it's up to your steady hands and clear eye.

So, question. What calibres deliver sufficient punch accurately at four hundred yards? I think that the thirty thirty has to be ruled out as it lobs too much. It's hard to calculate range in some situations, such as across a steep valley where much of the terrain in between is out of sight, and the point of impact of a thirty thirty bullet is vastly different at two hundred yards and three hundred yards. The punch it delivers is not able to be delivered accurately enough. I would also rule out the triple two except for the very good shooter and the professional who shoots all day, having little adrenaline in his system as he shoots and probably doesn't puff much on the hill. The light fifty to sixty grain bullet can be delivered accurately and does have enough punch, but only just, in my experience. Often deer hit with it won't fall instantly and tracking will be necessary which is fine unless the deer runs off into a wilderness of giant stinging nettle. That happened to me once and he took with him a tail that I wanted badly for my culling quota. So in my opinion the two four three is the lightest calibre suitable for deer. Interestingly enough the eighty five grain projectile hits harder at long range than the one hundred grain one. So from there on up almost all calibres will do the job.

The next question is, how much lead do you have to have flying through the air to down a deer effectively? Also how fast does it have to be going? I think that a minimum weight is about a hundred grains and a maximum is one hundred and fifty, on modern rifle calibers. Under one hundred grains means that some shot angles are not possible. For example, a running away from you angle. Less than a one hundred grain bullet in the rear leg of a deer is certainly not enough to drop it or even slow it down much. Unless the bullet has enough weight to penetrate to the vital organs in the chest of an animal from all angles it is insufficient in my book.

At the other end of the scale bullets of over a hundred and fifty grains that are doing sufficient speed to fly flat enough to give the desired accuracy over four hundred yards, simply hit too hard. You don't need the extra recoil at your end. Deer in the far distant mountains don't need the extra noise and the deer you shot doesn't need all that meat and skin damaged. I like efficiency and I like to believe that I am shooting with the best rifle available. I might not be shooting with the best rifle but I want to use the one that I believe is the best. I have more confidence that way. So I shoot better with that rifle.

Now I want to trim down the top end of the calibre range. To me the range of calibres from three hundreds up kick too hard, make too much noise and don't shoot flat enough. Of course some of the magnums shoot flat enough but the kick is even worse. For example lets fire two rifles pushing one hundred and fifty grain projectiles at the same muzzle velocity one of them being a three hundred caliber and the other a two seventy. At the muzzle of course they will be identical in hitting power and speed. However at three hundred yards the smaller diameter bullet will be traveling faster therefore hitting harder and it will not have dropped from the line of fire as much either. Air resistance is less. The recoil on both rifles will be approximately the same depending on the weight of the individual rifles. As the two seventy calibre delivers sufficient accurate punch why go bigger. To get the same punch at three hundred yards from a three hundred caliber you have to up the muzzle velocity and correspondingly the recoil and noise. There's simply no point to that.

So the range of deer rifles to my way of thinking is, calibre wise, between the two four three and the two seventy, two eighty range and, bullet weight wise, between the one hundred and one hundred and fifty grain projectiles. Above that there are some excellent rifle calibres, they just aren't deer rifles to me. They may be thar or wapiti rifles or bigger game rifles but here I am only talking about deer rifles and my own opinions of course.

So now, to carry on this nitpicking episode, which is what any defining of the best calibres in this range is, which calibre within this range is the best?

Well I think that depends on the person shooting and the kind of hunter he is. A hunter whose skill enables him to find most of his deer unalerted to his presence, will generally have more time to take his shot and be able to pick the angle that he wants on the animal, will do amply well with the two four three. The hunter that either finds his deer alerted to his presence, or spooked before he sees them, has to take shots from all angles and will probably do better with more power like from the two seventy or so calibres. But lets look at this a little closer, realizing of course that any calibre in this range will do just great.

The seven by fifty seven one hundred and fifty grain projectile has an excellent ballistic coefficient. In other words it acts exceptionally well in the air as regards wind effects and speed reduction. It has a highly efficient length and weight ratio for traveling through the molecules of our atmosphere. Likewise is the one hundred and sixty five grain three oh eight bullet but I have drafted out the three hundred calibres as deficient for what I think is best for deer. Remember this is my opinion only, and that as relates to confidence in the rifle that you have to shoot with.

Also another bullet that performs well is the two four three eighty five grain. Somehow these bullets shapes hold their speed better than others. If you analyze this you see that they have something in common. It is found in their length to diameter ratio. They are proportionally very close when compared to other calibres and bullet weights. Something in this ratio produces a fine performing projectile that holds its speed thereby retaining its hitting power and enhancing distance accuracy. So I think that the best calibres and bullet weights within those calibres are the ones that produce that ratio. Another one that produces that ratio is the six point five by fifty five in a one hundred and twenty to thirty grain bullet.

So lets look at four calibres. The seven by fifty seven in one hundred and fifty grain. The two seventy in one hundred and thirty grain. The six point five by fifty five in one hundred and twenty grain and the two four three in eighty five grain.

The first thing that we notice when looking at these rifles is that the two four three rifle has a shorter action than the others on many rifles. As the bullet is in the shorter size many manufacturers make a shorter action rifle and this gives a smaller and lighter rifle overall. This is an advantage to the hunter that carries his rifle all day for days on end, or the hunter that only hunts occasionally, and whose wrists aren't used to the weight. That is an advantage but may be offset by other things. The seven by fifty seven performs best with the one hundred and fifty grain bullets but is not so efficient with the one hundred and thirty grain bullets and less. Over distance they lose speed and power too quickly.

The two seventy is the same. The six point five by fifty five has a greater potential for the one hundred and thirty grain bullets. Loaded to its potential the six point five by fifty five may have a lesser muzzle velocity than the two seventy with the one hundred and thirty grains but at three hundred yards has retained more of

At Home in the Hills

its velocity so that it is faster than the two seventy and therefore hits harder and drops less at that distance. I say the potential for the six point five by fifty five not the actual performance that you will get from factory ammunition. Factory ammunition falls short of the potential for this calibre as there are so many old rifles of this sort around that loads up to the maximum would put some of those rifles in danger of over stressing.

I think that one hundred and twenty grains of lead flying at speeds of about twenty nine hundred feet per second at muzzle in this calibre would be very ideal for deer hunting for the average hunter. However factory loads for the six point five by fifty five only achieve about two thousand five hundred feet per second. Not enough to shoot flat and accurate over long distance.

A calibre that I am very interested in is the new six point five oh eight. It is also being known as the two sixty Remmington. It is essentially a three oh eight case necked down to six point five projectile. Not only is it able to achieve the two thousand nine hundred feet per second with a one hundred and twenty grain projectile it also has the shorter bullet case as does the two four three and so comes in a shorter and lighter rifle. It seems to me to be a very interesting calibre development. It even outstrips the seven millimeter oh eight in its ability to retain the hitting power of the one hundred and thirty grain bullet over distance. Another advantage of the six point five oh eight is that bullets will be available in all the same weights as the six point five by fifty five. A range that extends from one hundred grains to one hundred and sixty grains. The heavier ones would be useful for pigs, wapiti and thar too I would think. So that is some of my ideas on calibres. My personal choice is the two four three pushing one hundred grains at about three thousand feet per second. I have however been thinking very seriously about the six point five oh eight with one hundred and twenty grains at about twenty nine hundred feet per second.

A Few More Odd Deer

So, things that fly. Conjectures, guesses, suppositions and preferences. In the end the deer doesn't care what bullet he was killed with. What is absolutely important though is that the rifle that you have is one that you like, have confidence in, are used to, shoot well and are proud of. Put a good scope on it so that you can see that what you are shooting at isn't me or some other good keen bloke, and if you need glasses to drive be sure that you wear them when you're hunting. For the life of me I can't see how anyone can get, or have a rifle license, without having an eye test. Of course a person could mistake a person for a deer if he can't read a road sign. Make sure that the things that fly from your rifle fly true to the game that you are after.

However, the important thing is to be confident with the rifle you use, for that confidence will be the axle around which your best shooting revolves. No matter what rifle you have, if you, personally, are not confident in your, and its, combined ability to kill the game that you have presented in front of you, you will not shoot well and may not get the animal cleanly.

It's a personal thing what make and calibre of rifle that a hunter uses, and, apart from all the friendly banter about, it really is not the rifle that makes a hunter a good hunter or a good person to have as a mate either. No matter what kind of rifle you carry you have to find a deer before you can bring home the venison, and a good hunter will do better with a bow and arrow than a poor hunter with a three seven five H and H magnum. And a good guy with a blunderbuss who's never shot a deer in his life will be more welcome at my campfire than an arrogant cowboy with a successful hunting history.

Hunting isn't just about getting deer really, for me. Its about being there. But it is much better "being there" with a good rifle. One that gives you feelings that I'm sure Davy Crockett had for his Betsy or that Hawkeye attained with Killdeer.

CHAPTER TWELVE
The Hunter Becomes the Hunted

※

In 1970 I returned to Palmerston North one week day and walked into the Lands and Survey office where I spent some time working after leaving school, waiting until I was eighteen and was eligible to apply to become a deer culler. There was a particular guy there, Kevin Robinson, that I had really liked and respected - we had worked together a lot as we had both been Survey Assistant trainees.

After talking to my old boss for a few minutes I discovered that Kevin had died some months earlier from leukemia. It really knocked me. I asked where his wife and children were living and twenty minutes later was knocking at the door of a state house on the south side of town. I barely knew Denise. We had both been at a Public Services Ball some years earlier she reminded me - she with Kevin and me with a girl from the Post Office, a friend of my sisters. We had never really spoken to each other so when she answered the door there was an awkward silence for a few moments. It was awkward for several reasons. I was still reeling from learning that Kevin had died. I didn't know what to say to a widow of twenty two. She was in the midst of baking for a kindergarten day, had the kitchen full of cakes and flour all over her hands. Not a good situation to greet a grieving friend of her late husbands – and another reason that I will explain later.

After inviting me in, Denise made a cup of tea and before long I was playing with her children, Christopher and Amanda. Chris was then four and Amanda was about fifteen months. The afternoon passed quickly and when I left it was with a promise to write. I was living about three hundred kilometers away in Tauranga at the time.

Letters were slow in the writing but one that she wrote encouraged me no end and it was only a matter of months later that I was standing in the aisle of a church in Shannon watching her walk up to me. Dennys and Robin were my best men and we had about thirty friends, and relatives that I hardly ever saw, come around to my folks place for afternoon tea. Around that time Denise told me why it had been an awkward moment for her at the time we first met at the door. She said that she had had an unusual experience then. As soon as she opened the door a voice in her head said to her, "You're going to marry this man". It was a shock to her at the time and she was unable to communicate freely for a moment or two. I didn't know that that had happened for a long time. Just as well. I may have thought that she had been alone too much too.

It was to be my twenty first birthday the day following our wedding and I had on my first suit, a present from my parents. It still happens to be the only one that I have owned even yet. We planned the wedding around the time of the year. It was the first week of April. A good time for a hunter to get married. Our honeymoon wasn't to be the ordinary type.

The first day of our honeymoon we drove to Taihape and got into a motel there. They weren't over busy. The next day

Dennys arrived and we three headed out for the Otupae Station parking our car beside the road there and heading off up the farm track for the Mangaohane Plateau. It was a long slog for us as Dennys and I were carrying heavy packs and it was a hot day. We thirsted our way along with Denise's slim legs and brave smile leading most of the way. As we dropped down the zigzag onto the last stretch of tussock that gently angled up to Ruahine Corner Hut, the sun set on us. The plateau was quiet except for the occasional roar coming from the Makirikiri trig area and five deer that we spooked earlier had probably reached the safety of the small plateau peak called Aorangi if the pace that they were setting when we last saw them is anything to go by.

Denise's greatest fear was realized as we topped the last rise and saw a lonely light in the window of the hut. Someone else was there. We had hoped for solitude. However the two guys that greeted us, as we noisily opened the door of the hut and were cast in the sharp shadows of the Tilly lamp spilling it's light out onto the grass surrounding the hut, turned out to be really interesting blokes. One of them was Shorty Biddle and he was doing a trip from Hicks Bay to Wellington through the hills all the way. He was being accompanied by different guys who were doing stages of the walk with him. They left the next day after Dennys and I shot a curious and obviously sex mad stag just a few hundred yards from the hut half way to the airstrip. We had heard it roaring while we were having a cuppa just before the guys left. Dennys and I ran out and I roared it down closer before we dispatched it with his faithful Mannlicher .308 and my Sako 243. Now we had meat for the week.

Three Forestry guys, Henry Dorrian who I had worked for while I was culling a few years before, Ian Logan and Tom Cookson arrived after a few days and wanted the hut all to themselves - we noticed that they had some spotlighting gear

At Home in the Hills

hidden in their Landrover, not something that Forestry types were supposed to use. Ian benevolently drove us over to Scar and we dropped down to Makirikiri hut for the remainder of our honeymoon.

After arriving back from this trip I had to start looking for a job. It was only a day or so later that we noticed in the paper an advertisement for staff for the Manawatu Pest Destruction Board. They had a vacancy in Shannon. The foreman, a guy named Bob Bull with wavy hair and a ready smile, came to interview me. Not long after I was off to buy a single barreled shotgun, began scanning the pets and livestock column of the local newspaper for free dogs that looked like they might be suitable for rabbits, and looked for a house in Shannon that we could move into. I began working on the farms around the Rongotea area until Denise and I were able to rent the house we needed.

Then began the first years of our marriage as I followed many professional hunters before me. Deer hunting is not very conducive with marriage and the shift to rabbiting is a logical progression. The guys on the other rabbiting blocks of this part of the country were a mixed lot and a book could be written about them. There was Jimmy with his pack of dogs that mostly followed him around rather than fanning out into the cover ahead picking scents and flushing hidden rabbits. It was a surprise that those old graying dogs ever helped their master get any rabbits at all. Maybe Jimmy's kind heart drove him to do the dogs work for them. But, to be fair, when one of those gray haired, floppy eared, spaniel cross old timers stumbled across a hole in the ground that held a rabbit, after a lot of sniffing and snuffling their tails did wag faster, at least Jimmy said they did. And there always was a rabbit in there, at least Jimmy said there was.

Then there was Philip. He was the son of one of the builders of the Punga Hut and knew that area somewhat. He was a keen deerstalker and outdoorsman and a good shot with his pump action shotgun. The boss that we seldom saw was a guy named Ken Payne. He had been a culler on the North Western Ruahine block where I had been as well and had memories of hunting there in an era before ours.

Then there was Bob the foreman. I could never have guessed the influence that he was to have on my life. I really liked Bob. He was a clean living guy with a young family and he looked after his dogs extremely well. He and I had an interest, that wasn't encouraged by Ken Payne the boss, in whippet type dogs. Bob bred some pups from a pure bred greyhound to a whippet cross and they were really fast and we loved to watch them run. One that he gave me caught its first hare when it was still only a pup. They were great fun.

However the thing that was to change my life was the fact that Bob was a Christian. I had met some Christians before and wasn't very impressed, but Bob was different. He was also an excellent shot with his pump action shotgun. I saw him shoot two rabbits one day that were going in different directions with two shots that went off as fast as you can say Bang Bang. I can remember many shots that he pulled off that were no less than very impressive. However this Christianity thing that he was in to was a bit of a quandary.

During the months of lambing on the farms, all six of us from the southern Manawatu area gathered together to cover all the sandhills between Foxton and Tangimoana. A piece of land some thirty miles by about four miles following the coast. With our thirty odd snapping and snarling dogs in a trailer behind the Landrover we headed off early in the mornings. Usually our feet crunched off in the frost and we held our shotguns by the wood avoiding the steel parts that got sticky in the cold. It was a fun time with dogs running everywhere and rabbits panicking in all directions.

At Home in the Hills

Some of the dogs were buried there in the sand hills due to the odd wild pellet. We played five hundred all of the lunch times and generally got on well. One day we found a ball bearing that just fitted down the barrel of a shotgun and so we pulled the pellets out of a few cartridges and after wrapping the ball bearing in toilet paper and placing it in the empty front of the cartridges we fired it several times into a sand bank about a hundred yards away. It went surprisingly accurately. Also you could see it glint in the sun as it went.

Another day I was on a sand hill on one side of a shallow valley filled with lupin and long grass. Bob was standing on the other side of the valley and the dogs were going mad in between as a few rabbits were dodging about in the heavy cover of the lupins. Suddenly I was aware of a rabbit making its way up through the short and sparse maram grass on my side of the sand hill. Quickly my shotgun was up to my shoulder and I waited for it to appear again. There it was and before I could fire it erupted in a cloud of sand. Dumbfounded I looked up to see across the valley a smile that could have blocked out the sun on Bob's face. He had been watching the same rabbit and waited for me to see it and be almost ready to fire before he fired. He pulled that trick on some of the others too at different times. It was a lot of fun working for the Rabbit Board, or Pest Destruction Board to be more accurate. It left me time in the weekends to go deerstalking and for two years was a good job.

One day driving through Rongotea with Bob in the Landrover we passed a brick church. As we had been driving in silence for a time just to pass the time of day I asked, "Is that the church that you go to"? Bob laughed.

"No the church that we go to is a lot more fun than that place," he said.

Church! Fun! I had never heard those words used together.

Church and fun. Church had appeared anything but fun on the few times that I had poked my nose in to one of those places. Sombre. Serious. Scary. Echoey. Embarrassing. Yes, but never fun. We parted that day with Bob promising to bring along a tape recording of a church meeting for me to hear. I reluctantly agreed. It seemed to be important to Bob and Bob was a great guy. I wasn't going to turn him down on something that he was wanting to do so badly.

When he delivered the tape I took it home and listened to it. I really was surprised. It sounded just like one of the parties that my parents used to have at Linton when we lived there. There was always a lot of beer at those parties and it was just as well that some of the people only lived a short way from our place. Some of them must have thought they were driving along one of an identical set of roads as they left our place. Some had to be carried out to their cars. They were sometimes those kinds of parties and this church tape sounded like that. I was surprised. No, I was very surprised!

My life was changing quickly and before I knew it Denise told me that we were going to have an addition to the family. It turned out to be a son and we called him Matthew. I had always wanted a son called that, so it was a dream come true.

My rabbiting block was the Shannon one. It consisted of ninety thousand acres from Shannon to Linton and from the Manawatu River to the bush edge on the top of the foothills of the Tararua Ranges. It was the biggest one in that area. It suited me well as I was used to vast areas and any smaller block would have seemed limiting. It was also the only one that wasn't flat rising up to about a thousand feet or more on the eastern side. It wasn't real hills either but from the top I did get a taste of the expansive views that I was used to. I think that a hunter's eyes get used to long distance focus and flat land doesn't give that possibility. He

At Home in the Hills

gets frustrated on flat land.

One day, as a part of his usual routine, Bob came to spend the day with me on my block. He rotated this privilege with all of the guys and I think that he spent less time with me because he knew that I didn't need his company, or anyone's for that matter. I think that he did that also because we were striking up quite a friendship and he didn't want to be accused of favoritism. I didn't mind. I just enjoyed his company when he was there. The rest of the time my menagerie of dogs was company enough. They were always keen to go with me and walk as long as I did. They were devoted to me in a way no people had ever wished to be and they gave me so many laughs as the unusual happened so often.

Like the time that one of the greyhound type pups was chasing a pedigree Labrador bitch pup and the Labrador leapt into a dam full of water just for the hell of it. The brindle speedster following fast, hesitated for a split second that only someone that knew him would have noticed, and leapt after him. It was a very expressive split second. Full of, - what is that stuff? - will I? - she did - too late, here goes - wheee. It was a brave thing for the greyhound to do as he had never tried swimming before. He sunk! Straight to the bottom of the dam about four feet down. I could see him standing on the bottom looking around in confusion. I'm sure he had no idea where he was for that long drawn out moment or how he had got there. His head swished from side to side looking about in absolute surprise, and then he found his answer - he looked up. Up he came and splashed back to the edge with his ears down and a very sorry look on his face. I laughed and laughed and that only made his ears flatten even more as he skulked off with his tail between his legs. Dogs don't like to be laughed at.

Well this one particular day Bob came over the rise in the Boards Landrover a split second after I shot a rabbit racing up the fence line towards him. It was a wonder the Landrover hadn't collected a few pellets. As he pulled up I took the last few paces and picked up the rabbit, hooked an ear onto a barb of the top wire, and flipped the rabbit over it securing it there until it would turn into a dried stick in the coming weeks.

We hunted in that area of rolling hills all day and returned to the Landrover at lunch time. It was an overcast day and it seemed like the afternoon would be useless for hunting as rain started while we had lunch. Bob started talking to me about Jesus and Christianity again. He told me all about it. All...... about it! It took about two and a half hours and the afternoon was disappearing. The fact that the rain had stopped didn't seem to concern him. I think that he was enjoying himself. I was looking out the window feeling guilty about not being out there working, but then he was the boss. Who was I to feel guilty. I tried to seem interested and nodded when it seemed appropriate. Much of the conversation went past me in a bored haze but one thing that he said that day stuck in my mind like a hook in a doomed trout's mouth. Bob asked me a simple question. "Where does God fit into your life Mate?" I wrestled with that question for weeks. I couldn't answer it. The problem in answering it was that firstly I couldn't say that God didn't fit into my life even though it was true.

I had always said that I did believe there had to be a Being responsible for the existence of the universe, the earth and conscious life. What is life, where did I come from and for what purpose, had always been questions that had baffled me. That there had to be a purpose to it all was a settled issue in my mind. I still can't understand those who seem happy to live their lives with their only focus being the pursuit of career and building a comfortable environment to live and raise their families and then at the end of it all dying. There has to be a purpose to it that is bigger than that. Even spending as much time as possible following a recreation is, on its own, purposeless.

At Home in the Hills

To live with no answer to the question of why I am living, and to even be content with not knowing that, is surely the greatest example of an ostrich with his head in the sand that I can think of. An ostrich that thinks that it is a wonderful world under the sand and one that he wants to live in all of the time.

For me to say that God didn't fit into my life seemed to be a contradiction. If I did believe in a God behind it all and he was responsible for my existence then it would surely be an unforgivable neglect to not have him fit into my life somewhere. Yet he didn't fit into my life anywhere. But to say that and make it official was a step that I didn't want to take.

So the question trapped me in my own position. I couldn't say where God fitted into my life because he didn't fit anywhere, and I couldn't say that he didn't fit into my life because I felt that I was doing something very wrong not having the God who made me not fit into life in some way.

It made me mad that Bob had done this to me. It was even more of a pain in that I prided myself in having a reasonably high IQ and couldn't figure this dilemma out.

The upshot of it was that I deigned to go along to church with Bob one Sunday. At this time Denise became pregnant with Matthew and as she had never fully recovered from the years of nursing Kevin through his illness she had to spend the last six months of her pregnancy in the Palmerston North Hospital. I was living alone as the children were being looked after by friends, that I visited daily like I did Denise, and also had to go to work. It was not an easy time for us all. However I went to church one night with Bob.

It was a church that looked more like a hall set up to be a church. At the door a guy met me that remembered me from High School although I didn't recognize him. He wasn't the kind of guy that a hunter from the hills fitted with. His name, Percy, made it even worse. However he made me welcome and Bob and I found a seat in the back row and I settled in expecting an embarrassing time. My first surprise came when the singing started. The whole place erupted in song and the people were really into it. The only times that I had been to church, at cousins weddings and christenings etc., the singing seemed to be an exercise in who could sing the quietest. It was an embarrassment to endure. Everyone studied the lines of their songbooks as though they couldn't remember them and had to sing each word with full focus on its written form. Or they sung it gazing at the floor, the ceiling, the front of the church or at people that weren't looking at them. To catch the eye of someone while you were doing this super quiet singing was the worst. However here at this church of Bob's the singing was wild.

There was a guy up the front that was leading the songs and he had his eyes tightly shut, his head slanted toward the ceiling and was obviously singing to someone up there with intensity. He looked a little like an old time preacher that you might expect to step out of a western movie but it was clear that he was dead earnest. Then I noticed a little Maori woman by the aisle on the other side of the room. They were all singing a slower song and she had her eyes gently shut. The look on her face fascinated me. She was worshipping and I had never seen worship before. She was not just singing a song, she was loving and adoring a Being that she could either see or was feeling its presence. It was absorbing to watch.

That woman, and the man up the front I suppose in a more lighthearted way, were the two things that I took away with me from that night. Two sisters, dramatically dressed in black with heavy eye makeup on, sung some songs and a man spoke for some time but I wasn't impressed with them as I was with that woman. I guess I came away convinced that in the midst of these people God was not only known about but some of them knew him personally. I was interested.

CHAPTER THIRTEEN
New Horizons Open Up

Some weeks or a month or so later Bob asked me over to his place for tea again and proposed that he also invite some friends from Dannevirke as well - a town about forty miles away. Denise was able to come out of hospital for the night and so we duly turned up.

The couple were Ross and Shirley Davies and they had been 'in the Lord' for some years. We were learning a new lingo. They had come originally from Gore in the South Island and Ross had been an auctioneer and heavy drinker, evidently. They were nice people and we had a pleasant evening. I remember that Ross gave us an explanation that evening of the reason for the differing Christian denominations.

He told us the story of the Israelites leaving Egypt, crossing the Red Sea, winding their way for forty years through the desert enroute to the land God promised them which is now modern day Israel. He told us about the pillar of cloud, that was the presence of God with them, that lead them, showing them where and when to move. The pillar of cloud in the day became a pillar

At Home in the Hills

of fire at night so that at all times they could see it. However the significance of it was that the people were to always to stay with the presence of God. However, he said, at times during the forty years their camping places were probably really nice and they stayed there for some time before the pillar moved on and they had to pull up camp and move to follow it. When this happened, Ross continued, there would have often been some that found it harder to move on as they had come to like the place where they were and wanted to stay there. So the cloud of the presence of God moved and an encampment of people stayed.

They were still Israelites but they weren't living in the presence of God anymore. He surmised that this could have happened often as the people moved around in the wilderness for forty years.

Then he enlikened these 'stayers' to many of the denominations. Many of the denominations were once right in the presence of God and God was evident amongst them. They had the pillar of cloud and of fire, so to speak.

The Roman Catholic Church was at one time the only church and there were among them people that really knew God and whom God really worked through. The Methodist church, founded by John and Charles Wesley, really moved with God in its early years. Thousands of people that heard John Wesley preach heard him as the voice of God to them and the whole of England and the Americas were changed during that time. The Salvation Army had the presence of God with them when William Booth, the founder, and others of his contemporaries began it last century. The Pentecostals of the early twentieth century were the same. And so many of these denominations were founded by God as he moved in the days of their beginnings.

It is not that God has left them, Ross told us, because they are God's people, it is just that the revealed presence of God has moved on and something of the organization left has become an encampment around a lifestyle that developed when the presence of God was there. He finished by telling us that presently the cloud of God's presence is moving again and churches all over the world are experiencing His power, miracles and living teaching again. The church that Bob and his wife Christine go to was one of them. Remembering the Maori woman's face at church that night that I attended left me in no doubt of that. It was obvious that she at least knew God personally.

So in the midst of those times when Denise was in hospital and I was working for the Rabbit Board, alone most of the day, I began to read books that other people were writing of their experiences near the cloud of God's presence.

I have always been quite a reader and in the huts all over the Tararua and Ruahine Ranges bad weather always drove me into the depths of sleeping bag while I devoured the books there. I must say that most hunters are not readers of the classics. Westerns were the main diet and some of the more unsavory magazines. I devoured them all as I have not been able to see a written word without checking it out. Spelling mistakes have always jumped off the page at me even when I wasn't reading the page. I can see back now that the Lord was behind all of this time of my life. It is as if He was overseeing all of the influences coming into my life. Bob especially. He was such a fine guy and I could see that God was real to him.

One day while we were talking about Jesus and Christianity and the discussion was getting quite involved - I was trying to sort it all out - Bob said something else that affected me immensely. It still does till today. I guess I was trying to understand what Christianity was like for Christians, what God was like and how do you "be" a Christian. What do you do to know God? Bob said to me simply, "You can't find God in your mind, mate.". He stumped me there. I had always found that my mind was the tool that I used to sort out all kinds of problems. I had done well at school and had a bright future if you could believe my teachers. I had loved mathematics because with your mind you could work out the answers to difficult problems and find the one and only answer. I had enjoyed that. Now Bob was saying that I couldn't use my mind to analyze and discover Christianity. He was saying God is not a concept that you can master. You can't learn all about Him and therefore become a Christian. Being a Christian is knowing God. Just as knowing all about anyone is not knowing them. Knowing them involves contact. You can't find God with your mind, only with your knees, so to speak.

Here I came to the big issue for everyone in becoming a Christian. It means praying in such a way that you surrender yourself to His presence. Coming into the presence of God after we die is something that we all will have to face compulsorily. We have no option then. But to do that voluntarily is another thing. I really wrestled with that. What is God like? What will happen to me if I come into His presence? Bob had assured me that Jesus loved me so much that He died on the Cross for me. That is a lot of love, I thought. So I wasn't afraid that He would do anything to me. He hadn't in the twenty one years of my life so far and so I didn't think that He would start now.

The issue was what would He expect of me. I mean if He was willing to come into my life on what grounds could I come into His? I guess that I knew that there was only one way that I could come. I knew that to meet God I would have to surrender all of my life to Him from that point on. It would mean that I would have to put my life so much into His hands that I would become personally and do practically whatever He would ask of me for the rest of my life. This was not a big ask. This was the ask of my life. This was a huge ask! There was nothing greater that could be asked of me.

All of the questions went through my mind. How would my life turn out if I did this thing? What would my friends think? Would my life be enjoyable? Would I be considered a religious crank? Some of the people at the church certainly were considered that. I even thought some of them were. However those were the unreal ones not the genuine people that I could see knew God. What would my parents think? And so on and on my thoughts went as I weighed up this decision.

Learning and believing that God loved me, that He knows me better than I know myself, He made me after all, I was confident that any changes He made in my life would be better than ones that I could make. I could never consider that a Being that could make such beauty as the earth and the skies, the mountains and the deer in them could have a bad bone in His body. If my friends could not accept me deciding to be a Christian could I let that stop me from fulfilling my obligation to my Creator? I only had two or three real friends not counting the sparse trail of girlfriends that I went to dances and the movies with in those days, and so this was a real consideration. Those friends, Dennys and Robin and their father and family were very important to me, and still are. The issue was what would they think? I finally decided that the friendship that we had would weather anything and it has. They would not stop loving me as a friend no matter what path I took in life.

The only issue I was left with was of course the main one. Could I give my life to God? Could an independent, freedom loving, footloose, loner, hunter and man of the mountains give his life to God to be whatever He wanted and designed? Could I give the rest of my days to a path that could lead me anywhere? Could I give myself and all that I had become to Hands that may redefine my personality and change my nature into something else that I was not familiar with?

At Home in the Hills

If God is my Creator, I thought, then He has a plan for my life that will be more fulfilling than I could possibly find myself. He can be trusted. He is goodness itself. He will never let me down. Not only will He guide me into a life that will be better for me than I could find but He will also live it with me. That was the big draw card. I found that I really wanted to know God like that Maori lady at the church. There was something in the eyes of some of those people that really drew me. I wanted to have what they had.

So the day arrived. I didn't know when I woke up that day, that it was, the day. I just thought that it was another difficult day as all of the other ones at that time had been. I went to work all day and in the late afternoon drove to Palmerston North Hospital to see Denise. We spent an hour or so talking at her bedside and then it came my time to leave. I had arranged to drive over to Rongotea to have tea with Bob and Christine in the evening before heading back to Shannon and the cold lonely house that hadn't seen any heating in it as I was away a lot. But then I was used to no heating in the huts that I had lived in and I was still living a bushman's life. I still wore black woolen singlets, woolen socks, woolen shirts, had hunting gear strewn casually around the house and had a stag skin on my bed as a cover.

Tea with Bob and Christine was uneventful and I don't know if we even talked about the Lord that night. It happened on the way home. It was about eleven o'clock and the night showed no moon due to the overcast sky. The lights of the car picked up the posts along the roadway and the dashes of white along the centre of the road rushed at me and flashed under the car as I sped along without much thought of anything except getting home and hitting the sack.

I slept well in those days because of my youth but even more so because of the outdoor exertions of walking for at least eight hours every day. In the weekends I took time off from work and went deerstalking. I came back to work for the rest of only walking on flat land.

Somewhere about twenty miles from home my thoughts came to focus on the decision that I had before me of surrendering my life to God and giving myself to walk with Him the rest of my days. Slowly the feeling of importance over this decision intensified until it took on another dimension altogether. I was suddenly aware that I was not fully alone anymore. There was a strong sense of the silence being a living silence. Similar to that feeling of being watched. Similar to that feeling you get walking into a clearing and there being another presence there, a sense of the deer that had just departed before you arrived. But this was more so than any of those. I knew that I was being watched and I knew who it was although I didn't know Him then as I do now. It was the presence of Jesus, right there in the car. He was waiting for me. He was waiting for me to make the decision.

So it had to be made now. I didn't need to know anything more about it. I knew enough. To put my life into the hands of the One who made me, loved me and had a purpose for my life that He wanted me to live out. A purpose that I would never know unless I first committed to it. Even then it would only be revealed bit by bit as I walked it out. I knew that God didn't want me to know what His purpose for me was so that I could go off and do it all by myself. He wanted to live it with me and so to stave off the possibility of me going off and doing it my way alone He would only reveal it to me part at a time so that I had to keep in contact with Him all along the way. His desire was for me to live my life with Him closest to me all the time. It seemed a dream come true to be able to live my life with God but there was a natural hesitation that I'm sure everyone would have in surrendering their life to another, even one so good as God.

At Home in the Hills

The miles were slipping by as I wrestled with the decision and the presence of Jesus waited patiently with me. The tension in me rose as I realized that I had to make the decision before I reached home. I didn't know if Jesus would come inside the house when I got there. It was such a mess due to no housekeeping being done for so long. The tension rose and rose. Finally I did it. In a simple way I responded by saying all that was necessary. The question was really a yes or no, one. Yes, I would give my life to Jesus by asking Him to come into it, or no, I wouldn't ask Him to come into my life and take over. Finally I said the words right out loud that I have never regretted and have been so thankful to have had the opportunity to have said.

OK Lord, come in.!

I'm sure the presence smiled but very soon I was alone in the car again and it seemed like it had been a dream. I pulled up in the drive at home and went inside to bed without really considering the happenings along the way.

The next morning, just before dawn, I rose and dressed, downed my breakfast of eight or ten Weetbix and drove out the few miles to where I kept my dogs. They were housed in kennels at a small gully just north of Shannon called Brick Hill. I let them all loose and they tore around the place trying to get a quick bite from the cow legs that hung there before being told sternly to get into the boot of the car.

There were dachshund crosses, beagle crosses, spaniel crosses, foxhound crosses and greyhound crosses amongst the mob of canine friends that I had. All of them were characters and I loved them all. We spent the days together doing what we all loved. Roaming open country and hunting. They all jumped into the trunk except Trixie, the little toy terrier of some kind crossed with a dachshund. She was too small to jump up into the boot of the car but could go into tiny places to rout out rabbits that the others couldn't. I lifted her up gently with my boot and she found her curling up place between the legs of the others all entwined into the cramped trunk. Slowly I let down the lid and closed it with a click.

Ten miles away I pulled up in front of a gate on Kaihinau Road where I would spend the day rabbiting. As the lid of the boot opened again the dogs spilled out like a waterfall and began racing around cocking their legs on the fence posts of the roadside, scratching the long grass with their feet and sniffing everything, already searching for last nights passing rabbit. I leaned into the car and pulled out my single shot shotgun propping it against the front door handle where it wouldn't fall over. Then I wrapped my hunting belt around my waist filling the shot loops with purple colored, regulation, Rabbit Board cartridges – number fours. Grabbing a canister of cyanide flakes I filled my aluminium bottle that fitted onto my hunting belt. Then the folding spade, with which I filled in rabbit holes after I had thrown some of those cyanide flakes into it, slipped into a loop on my belt too. The dogs were always impatient to get going in the morning and so was I.

My fit legs threw me over a rickety wooden gate that had a broken hinge at the bottom and the dogs squirmed through the wires of the roadside fence fanning out into the farmland with its tantalizing smells; heaven for a dogs nose. I followed them quickly falling into the stride that has taken me over hundreds of miles of high mountain ridges and rough back country.

There was no warning. Before I had gone twenty yards suddenly the world changed. An amazing thing occurred. I raised my eyes in wonder and looked up and the sky was bluer than I had ever seen it. The lush grass that I was walking through suddenly exploded with greenness. The hills, a mile or so to the east, sloping up a thousand feet, leapt in wonderful clarity to a beauty that I had never seen before. I marveled as I realized that the ground that I was walking on felt like six inch thick marshmallows and I felt so light. I felt like I was floating I felt so light. And inside an amazing feeling came. I had never felt anything like it. I cannot describe it. However the best way to give an indication of how it affected me is to say that I had a feeling of absolute certainty that everything would be all right for me from that moment on. Later I learned that it was the peace of God come into my heart. I also learned later that the feeling of lightness was because of the burden of my sins taken away.

We don't realize how heavy the burden of our guilt is, due to sins that we have committed against God, and others. When it lifted from me I felt like my feet were barely touching the ground. I was born again as the Bible describes in the book of John chapters one and three. It was no psychologically hyped response to an emotional situation. It came by surprise while I was completely alone in a familiar situation. It was God coming to me. Just me.

The day was a wonderful day. I was changed and the change was wonderful. I don't know how many rabbits I got that day or even if I got any. It didn't matter to me. I walked all day in a new realm and it was so exciting to know that it wasn't going to evaporate away. It was a new life beginning. It was the beginning of a new life. I sung all day inside my mind. I tried some of the songs that I had heard them sing at church when I went but couldn't remember them very well. But I did know 'Amazing Grace' and 'How Great Thou Art', so I sung them. They went through my mind for weeks and I didn't really know that I was worshipping God as I sung them. I was just really full of happiness, feeling so accepted by God, and so grateful. I think my face looked like that Maori lady's face.

I had been given a small New Testament at high school when

New Horizons Open Up

I was in the third form and had tried to read it but not found it very interesting at the time. Now I dug it up from somewhere and took it to work each day hidden in my shirt pocket. At lunch times – which I have to admit sometimes dragged out to more than an hour – I would find a suitable tree or clump of rushes and settle down and read it. The dogs would collapse too in the sun and we made a silent companionship there as I read and read and read. The words were different now. They seemed to give me, again and again, the feelings of peace and awesome vision of my surroundings that spoke of God to my heart.

Over the months that remained of my time working for the Manawatu Rabbit Board I read that New Testament over maybe fifteen times or so. I loved reading it. I must have made an unusual picture with my hair long and in a ponytail due to the friends that Denise and I had made on the fringes of the drug scene. I wore a band around my head made of a slinky skin that I had got from the upper Maropea area while culling a few years before and the Shannon farmers and people that lived there found me a bit strange I'm sure.

Some weeks later I was baptized in water and then with the Holy Spirit and my new Christian life took on an even greater reality.

I was on a path now that was not unlike the tracks in the mountains. Usually upward. Containing times when you can't see very far ahead and have to just put your head down and slog it out. Arriving suddenly without warning on a peak with magnificent views making you realize the height gained and ground covered in the trees. Edging past dangerous bluffs where you have to walk carefully and resting in the evenings with good company, eating a meal that you appreciate more than usual in the light and warmth of a good fire.

A fire in the mountains always gives a place a sense of home. A fire is a constant source of fascination and, as all men of the outdoors know, can be gazed into for hours on end. It is the life of a campsite, the warmth of a place of rest, the source of good food, the source of light to see by and the place where company is enjoyed to the fullest. Just so is the Holy Spirit in the Christian life.

I told Denise what had happened to me and she was excited for me. Eventually she came to give her life to the Lord and had her experience with Him too. We ended up feeling that the Lord wanted us to have a future in the ministry as full time preachers, teachers and counselors so we ended up going to a Bible School on Great Barrier Island for a few years.

Now our lives, following the Lords purposes, have had many adventures. We have been taken to many countries of the world to tell of our experiences with God and to tell people what we have learned from Him. The road of the Lord has been rocky at times but He has always been there and even the hard times have had their reasons. The wonderful thing has been that He has always been there. He is the wonderful friend that sticks closer than a brother.

My life as a hunter was the foundation of my manhood. Finding the Lord as a real life Friend and Guide, Teacher and Master, Father and Enabler, has been the fulfillment of all of my existence.

I owe so much to other hunters. Bob Bull, my foreman on the Rabbit Board, is second to top of the list. On the top is God who hunted for me and found me and has shot me full of His love.

I stopped going into the hills for a few years as I sorted out my priorities. Hunting had been my life and I had devoted myself to it with a love and intensity, that I began to realize, should only be given to my Creator. Hunting and the mountains had been the place where I had sought meaning for my existence and satisfaction for my soul. Lacking something better it was not a bad way to do that. Better than how some youths try to fill that

New Horizons Open Up

need with drugs, parties, crime, fast cars or unrestrained sex. Any sport is a better thing to be involved with than that.

However none of those, even sport, can actually fill the need for meaning and satisfaction we all have inside us and which we all try to fill with some activity. The need for meaning and satisfaction is a craving within us that youth feel the most. As we get older, and find no answer to the ache that unmet craving releases, we become dulled to its pain and it merges into the many pains that we experience in life. We then can't isolate that pain anymore and aren't aware of it the same. Only finding our Creator through Jesus Christ gives that meaning and satisfies us in the deepest place of our soul. It is obvious that being creations of God we cannot find fulfillment without Him. Anything that we pursue to seek that fulfillment from will get in the way, in the end, of knowing the Lord as that fulfillment. So I gave up the mountain life expecting that I would never go into the mountains again. I devoted my life to doing whatever the Lord wanted of me.

Then one day the Lord said to me to go into the mountains and take my son Chris with me. We spent six days in the Pourangaki River valley in heavy snow. We had a wonderful time and I discovered that a part of me - maybe the fiber of my manhood - was sculptured there. It is the nearest thing that I have to a home in this world.

Since then I have regularly returned to these old haunts and homes in the hills. It is where I am me. Where my God walked with me when I didn't know it. Where the beauty that He created, and which is an expression of His own nature, was built into me and has become a foundation of my life. From that foundation He has built a life, that, never being untrue to it, has extended horizons around the globe and beyond. What a wonderful God we have. What a wonderful world He has made for us to enjoy

At Home in the Hills

and what a wonderful life He has made for each of us but which we only find when we kneel to Him, asking His forgiveness for our sins and putting Him in His rightful place as our Creator, Master, Lord and Father.

Chapter Fourteen
Changes in The Hills

I lift my cup up to my lips for a last sip and find, of course, that the tin mug is long since emptied. The sun has risen well in the sky too and the day is warming up. It is now some hours since my bath in the frost of the morning and I came to sit under this tree here at Waterfall Creek hut in the headwaters of the Kawhatau River. Emerging, as from a dream, the flats of the river stretching northwest downstream towards Crow hut and the Mokai Patea Range, come into focus, shimmering in the sun. What wonderful places, people and events are stored away in my memory. There is so much more too that comes back to mind from time to time. The hills. Hunting the red deer. Campsites and comrades. Tussock and bush, river and rain. I'm so at home in the hills and thankful to God my Father for it all.

I lean on the tree that has supported my back, and stagger to my feet. As I walk back to the hut, under the refreshing shade of the beech trees to replenish my cup, my legs feel stiff with sitting for so long. The hut fire is all white ashes until I rummage around in it with a stick, revealing a few red hot coals. A handful of twigs and a puff of breath rekindle it and soon the billy is boiling again and another cup of tea is steaming away in my mug. This is one of the places that I came to and loved over thirty years ago. It is almost exactly the same and yet it is different to me as well.

In one way the hills change only slightly and imperceptibly over the years, and in another way they change quickly and massively.

When I first started hunting years ago, a particular hunting spot that almost always held a deer or two consisted of a few clearings on a ridge that climbed gradually out of secondary-growth bush. These clearings were interspersed with scrub that hid the deer that I hunted, and myself as I hunted them. The ground was covered in broad-leafed grasses that dried to a light tan in the summer heat and aged and rotted in the winter, but these gave me easy access along the ridge, making travel there a real pleasure. I and my friends sat there in the sun often with binoculars, glassing the surrounding ridges that were like this one, and we saw and shot quite a number of deer in that area.

Recently I returned there after many years of absence, arriving on a windy day when the cloud was limiting my view to no more than thirty to forty yards. I popped out of the bush pushing through the last few yards of leatherjacket onto the ridge, not sure exactly where on the ridge I was appearing. I still didn't recognize the part of the ridge I was on when I saw what I could through the low cloud cover from the top of it either. I thought for a moment that I may have made a mistake and be on some other ridge that I hadn't been on before. However, this ridge had been the one that I had frequented often in years gone by, and I know that I have something of a photographic memory for past hangouts of mine and the hills and creeks that lead to them. After taking a moment to think, I knew I had not made a mistake.

So I headed down the ridge in the murk of gale driven cloud,

Changes in The Hills

pushing hard through the knee- to waist-high leatherjacket. Suddenly, a rock jutting above the brittle and unrelenting stiffness of the scrub, that many a hunter will not venture into, caught my eye. It was now crowded to the base with growth that did not use to be there twenty eight years ago when I used to use it as a backrest. Its familiar shape had not changed and it felt like I had returned to an old friend. One though, that had suffered through the years that I had been away with a thousand storms and a thousand changes of weather and the imperceptible onslaught of growth on the hillside around it.

Looking at it, I saw again the familiar lumps and hollows as they always had been, roughly spotted with white lichens. It was a sad day traveling that ridge that had once been so wonderful to hunt, but was now a real challenge to walk along for its two to three foot growth of rough and spiky leatherjacket that tore at my legs and scratched me badly. I wonder if I will ever return. Next time it may have growth to head height. The place had changed and was changing, but it was still the same too. I snapped a short stick of dead and dried leatherjacket and put it in my pocket. Later, back in the Punga Hut, I whittled it into a rough cross and now wear it round my neck.

One time, walking up the Pourangaki River, the riverbed was so full of gravel that you had to duck to walk under the wire bridge at the Pourangaki hut in the middle reaches of the valley. Then a flood removed all that shingle, and now the bridge is fifteen feet or more above your head from where you stand under it. The whole river length is now harder to negotiate because of the deep holes and large rocks that the consistent fickleness of the water flow itself first caresses, and then can blast with a power that can only be wondered at.

Landslides, plant growth, floods, deer numbers and the like change the hills at an imperceptible rate that we mostly don't notice over a short time. Photos of the hills, silhouettes of a hundred years ago, are still recognizable to us today. The weather doesn't have the power to rapidly change the overall, except after the effects of thousands of years.

However, there is another type of change that takes place about the hills that is much more dramatic, although not physical. It concerns the way we each perceive the hills as we change throughout our life's development, both personally and in the society which changes around us.

A simple example is the change to the mystery every explorer of last century faced, and that was completely lost with the invention of the aeroplane. Think about it. When there were no maps and no ways to know what was over the distant peaks on a hazy horizon, except by going there to have a look for yourself, the hills were a different place for men to consider and be in. There were no aerial photos or satellite pictures that can pick up a matchbox, with their eagle eyes, in space. What the hills meant to those explorers they will never mean to any person again. The same hills we can go to today are a totally different place to us than they were to the likes of Mr. Explorer Douglas, the great discoverer of much of the Southern Alps of New Zealand in the last century. We can never experience them as he did. They are as different a place to us as the moon is to our back yard. Yet they are also the same places, with only imperceptible physical changes.

In the same way, only two men ever went to the top of a particular Mount Everest, or Chomolungma as it is known by those who have lived with it longer. Only Sir Edmund Hillary and Tenzing Norgay knew, and ever can know what it was like to climb up that last ridge of Everest from the South Peak. That ridge and final summit as they knew it at the time, with its mystery, reputation of unclimbability and mankiller, and history of failures, ceased to exist when they returned and framed the renown words to another, "We knocked the b---------- off." It has never been, and never will be the same, for any other. The mystery had gone, the reputation had changed, the fear level had dropped and, for any other being it could never feel like it did for those champion mountain climbers and fortunate men. They knew Mount Everest as no one ever will again.

Mount Aiguille in the European Alps is another example that has captured my imagination, although every place changes as human perception changes and social developments occur. This mountain for centuries was known by the people that lived at its base, or in sight of it, as an unclimbed and unclimbable mystery in their midst. No one knew what lay on the huge grassed plateau which gradually sloped to a pyramid peak at its extreme end. Because of the mystery of its summit, these people lived in its shadow with an awe of it that permeated their lives, and it affected every aspect of their existence in some way. It is different to live with a mystery towering over you every day than to live without that.

That is why we must learn to dream up continually new challenges, because we keep accomplishing the ones that we have and it leaves us dreamless, an unbearable state of being. And sometimes the possession of a dream can be better than the accomplishing of it. One day it dawns on us that every dream that we accomplish means one dream less that we have.

This powerful mystery of Aiguille Mountain affected even those people who lived and died miles away from the sight of the mountain, as it gave the people of the area a focus for national pride. Then one day in 1492 Julien de Beaupre and two priests climbed it. He and his companions found, amazingly, that there was a significant herd of chamois living on the wide and grassy plateau. Another mystery that is yet unsolved I think. The climber had to stay on the summit plateau until the King of the

At Home in the Hills

country sent an emissary to see them up there, and verify that they had indeed conquered it. From that day on, the mountain was different to human experience. It was looked at differently. It was not the unclimbable mystery that it had been. It had changed as far as mankind was concerned, and it would never be the same again. In fact, every time it is climbed by another climber for his first time it will change massively for that person, and a little bit more for all.

The last poem that I have included in this book starts off the first two lines stating that this fact has affected me too. The hills that I first went into as a youth haven't changed much, really, but I have. The way that I experienced them as a young man growing into adulthood is, in essence, gone. It has been replaced by another level of experience of them, but it is in fact quite different. Sometimes I get a whiff of the past as I knew it at an unexpected moment. Looking at the ranges from a distance, a photograph, or a moment in conversation with someone, it may happen, but it is impossible to hold onto. It is a momentary descending of an old atmosphere, smell, feeling or sense that either brings back the past in a tangible way or transports me back into it, I don't know which.

Philip Holden, the author of many hunting books, asked me recently if I had any colour photos of the Ruahines, that we both hunted in the sixties, for a book that he was writing then. I said that I took only black and white photos in those days but do have some recent ones in color that have no modern aspects to them. He rightly replied that recent photos don't have the essence of the sixties era in them even though they show the hills almost exactly as they were then. Perhaps we unconsciously discern the difference in the sixties processing of colour film from the present, more perfected systems. Perhaps there was something more mystical in the sights the hills gave in the sixties that the eye of the sixties hunter can pick up in the old photos, but can't see in the modern ones. I don't know, but his reply was a true one.

We change, technology changes, society changes and, although the hills remain much the same, hunting, tramping and the experience of wilderness changes. It is different for us, and oh do I often mourn the loss of the days of yore. This poem speaks of this mourning.

The Unknown Tentcamp

There is a fork in the Unknown Stream
Where once a Tentcamp stood.
A secluded home for wandering cullers,
The chimney, axed slabs of wood.
A canvas camp oft which I dream
'Neath virgin beech, grand and pure.

Dennys and I stayed one April night,
In our bags on hard ground we retired.
Blue ducks whistled gaily outside, below,
Drifting wearily, us and the fire.
Minding the day yet again back and fro
As the hail laden air 'gan to bite.

We'd seen two then got one 'for the big stag was heard
So we'd done pretty well up till then.
But that stalk and that stag and his bellowing roars,
Years have passed but my pulse still quickens.
Savoring the ranges and their rugged rich stores,
We slipped slowly to sleep our souls stirred.

At Home in the Hills

> *The fork in the Unknown streams still the same*
> *But the camp is gone now, overgrown.*
> *An old chimney slab unnoticed rots there,*
> *The old antler says time is to blame*
> *For the pang in my heart as a dear mountain home*
> *And an era is gone without peer.*

The social attitude towards rifle ownership is changing and that affects us hunters deep inside, and so affects the whole experience of hunting. Where I grew up, as I have already said, rifles were a part of every farmer's life and most houses would have had at least a twenty two in the wardrobe or the master bedroom, or in the broom cupboard at the back door. Now there is a sneering in the eyes of many who believe that it is a horror to shoot animals.

One person complained to me once, "How can you shoot such a beautiful thing as a deer?" I replied, "Do you eat lamb? Have you ever been to the slaughter house of a freezing works? There the men stand ankle deep in a sea of blood with their arms swinging continuously, a lamb ending its life each swing. They are your hands preparing your meal. The death of a deer on a mountainside is a much cleaner thing than that."

And, if they say, "No I don't eat meat I am a vegetarian," I say, "Do you use fly spray? Have you seen the agony of a Blowfly trying to escape the effects of it with it's dying mania? Is a fly's death less important because it is smaller, or uglier, or a nuisance? Is a deer's death bad because the deer is beautiful? Is the value of a life greater because of the beauty of the being? That is the mentally that Hitler had. Do you kill mosquitos that bite you? Is it all right to kill something that happens to have to inconvenience you to live itself, and wrong to kill something that doesn't inconvenience you?" Is your inconvenience the balance of an animals life or death?

The fact is that the killing of animals, by other animals and ourselves, is a part of nature's balance and is a part of life for all humans. Has city life, which can be very sterile in its removal from nature, so removed us from certain life and death realities that we now reject nature's values? If it has we may destroy nature from ignorance, believing that we are saving it. That doesn't mean that we should not look after the animals that we have left on this planet. Every extinction is a terrible catastrophe and must be avoided at all cost short of the loss of human life. But hunting is a basic inheritance to us all from antiquity and, given the right governing of firearms, care of our natural environment and nurture of all species, cannot be taken away from the average citizen.

Hunting, and the challenge of the hills, has kept many a boy from a wild and destructive youth, and almost always developed in him values and character that has helped him become a valuable asset to society. The mountains teach a person commitment to a goal. You often have no alternative other than to persevere when the going is tough. They teach rewards for effort spent.

The views and beauty of nature are much richer to the person who is immersed in it, in raw physical oneness, rather than the luxury traveler observing from a comfortable cultured observation point of some sort. The mountains teach a person to make decisions seriously, as many of the decisions made there are life and death ones. Foolishness is penalized severely.

Time in the hills will give a person self-confidence and individual reliability because when there, even with others, your survival is all up to you. Tramping will draw a type of person, and hunting will draw another type and it has its place. Hunting differs in that it gets a person under the skin of the hills in their vast magnitude to an intimate observation of the mountains, the bush and the rivers at close range. A closer range than a magnifying glass can attain, for over time the hunter notes every facet in the varied details of many environments and links occur that tie nature as one entity.

The hunter alone finds the forbidding nooks and crannies that no one else would go into without good reason, and often to the hunters own frustration, but he still spends time there. He experiences more of it than others. The hunter also sees his own part in it all as a vital link, and may be lucky enough to find his home in the hills. I dread to think how I would have gotten on through the tumultuous years of my youth, if I hadn't had the hills and the call of the deer in them to occupy me then. The hills and my manhood are linked.

I have taken groups, as I will be in a few days time, of mostly city bred young people, and older ones too, into the bush for five and six day tramps over the last ten years. It has been wonderful to see the things that they have encountered in the hills and in themselves during those times. It has been entertaining for us all in different ways and I have enjoyed being a part of their particular development into the adult world. Of course, the only way to really live as an adult is if you retain childlike attitudes of wonder, freedom and humor amidst the compulsory demands such responsibilities as family and work enforce. The hills give the greatest opportunity for that and will return their blessing on an individual who knows how to live there.

However the point of what I am trying to say here is that public opinion about firearms and hunting, misinformed as it is, does have an effect on our mindset that wasn't there in my young days and so has changed the experience of hunting today.

But probably the biggest change to the hills in my lifetime has been the development and wide use of the helicopter. Now places that were inaccessible to all but the very fit and adventurous, who were willing to expend days of energy to get to a chosen spot, can be invaded by anyone with enough money in just minutes from considerably large towns. It used to be that the weekend hunter or the once a year hunter was only found in easy to get to places around the farm bush edges of the ranges, or short distances up the open valleys. You could normally tell who had gone up a valley or along a track in front of you, and so often had an idea of how many people were in the area that you were hunting, or if anyone was at the hut that you were approaching.

Now you can find anyone anywhere. They drop out of the sky. They come with their alcohol, gas cookers and over-supply of ammunition too, and that makes a difference to life around the hut or campsite at night. It makes a difference to how you feel sneaking along in the bush the next day too. They come with their flabby white legs, their beer guts, and their overconfident talk and attitudes as well. It used to be when you met a bloke way back in the bush you could be pretty sure that you were meeting a reasonable type of guy. Now all the diversity of the race can be facing you and sharing a valley with an unsavory sort is no fun. It just ain't what it used to be.

Now don't get me wrong here. Ninety five percent of the hunters that I have met in the hills have been a pleasure to meet, and I have enjoyed those moments on the track pausing to talk. Pausing at another's camp for a brief shooting of the breeze, as I have been slogging up the valley to a distant destination, has always been an enjoyable respite on the trail too. Almost always those who have dropped out of the sky into the country that I have been in have been great blokes that I have been glad to have met. I have shared my knowledge of the hunting spots there that I have known - if I have known any - often with what I have later thought may have been to my own future detriment. But I have shared those things because I have liked the blokes and have wanted them to have a good and successful time.

But now the other type, that we would all be better off without,

At Home in the Hills

can pop up anywhere too. That knowledge and occasional experience also changes the hills for us all. It was a thing that never happened. When looking at it all, as objectively as possible, things are different because of the choppers in many ways. And all of us are different people in the hills than we used to be too.

The Maropea Forks hut log book used to have only deer cullers names, messages and stupid comments and drawings in it. All of them added to the atmosphere of the place. They were the jottings of people that lived there for long periods and there was seldom a name that you couldn't identify from earlier in the book. The people that drifted around the hills there affected how you felt. They were a part of the place and you felt the effect of their presence. Now it is plastered with names only once written. It is a different person that frequents that wonderful place.

On my first arrival at Ruahine Corner Hut it was a wide expanse of remote tussock with mobs of ten or more deer still able to be seen feeding out in the late evening, or heading for the distant bush edge in the early light of dawn. It was a magic place. On another trip there much later there was a Rover car parked in front of the door! A bulldozed track had been pushed in just prior to our arrival. The scar of its presence, through the remote tussock of the plateau, was a desecration of that holy place and it remains so today. However, you would never get a Rover car to it now, or perhaps even a four wheel drive, without great difficulty due to the erosion of the wheel tracks through that limestone country.

The places don't change but the experiential essence of the hills does. Because this essence changes the hunters change. The eras come and go. The era of the Moa hunters was here and is gone. The era of the white explorer came and went. The era of the expansion of the deer herds under protection is over. The time of the great trophies and the intrepid hunters with their canvas tents, sports jackets, hobnail boots and three nought threes has

Changes in The Hills

passed, leaving us only photos and dusty heads on walls. The day of the skin hunting culler and the one hundred kills a day man is over. My prime time of the fifties to the seventies, golden and formative for me, has gone and this is another day now that I am lucky to be able to have health enough and fitness enough to be a part of. Where does the future go? I don't know as no one else does either, but my conversion to the spiritual reality and logical explanations of Christianity give me absolute hope in the future of the young. Young people and open spaces go together. Take the open spaces away from the young and they are lost and simply go to pack.

Well I'm glad that I went to pack as a youth. I went to pack my pack, as I will again in two days time, when I will wander off down the Kawhatau river to Crow hut, where I have a rendezvous planned with twelve trampers from Auckland. From there, we will climb over into the Waikamaka, Maropea and Mangatera rivers, for six days of adventure for them, and six more days at home for me. My roots are firmly imbedded here in these New Zealand mountains, and I will be found here whenever I am able and for as long as I am able. Downstream from here, near forty years ago, I learned to dive and swim underwater at a place called the Twin Bridges. The smell of this mountain range entered my nostrils then and has never left. Newton McConochie's words were true, "You'll learn no harm from the hills". But they didn't go far enough. You'll learn much good from the hills too.

My Sako in the corner of the hut and my old mountain pack are waiting their turn to be useful to me again. They are friends of my hand and back and nothing feels better than swinging along the mountain tracks with them.

The two days pass in glorious weather and on the morning of the third, at 6 a.m., I close the door of the hut. It has been another home in the hills for me, and, wandering over the flats that fill

At Home in the Hills

the spread out valley downstream from there, pack on back and rifle in hand, I disappear into the vast expanse of the Ruahines again.

Changes in The Hills

E<small>PILOGUE</small>

No the hills haven't changed where I roamed as a youth,
Pack, rifle, boots, Swanndri and friend.
With all that was needed right there on my back
And adventure around every bend.

I remember our young days in secondary growth bush
At the back of the Argylles farm.
We unconsciously learned the laws of the hills,
How to travel the slopes without harm.

Fresh deer tracks we saw and stories we heard,
Distant peaks and valleys beyond.
Our feet followed our hearts and dreams were attained
And the hills and I formed a fast bond.

I remember the long summer days they began
With a fire and brew before dawn.
Heavy dew on the ground and millions of stars,
Faint light on the ridge, a day born.

And the new day is welcomed by hundreds of birds
In full song on the tree'd river flat.
But before the light spreads the chorus is done,
In damp silence the mountains are wrapped.

As light spreads from the peaks to the low valley floors,
To the great trees and shag pile of fern,
The dew soaks the bush man, scrub tears at bare legs,
T'is nothing, maybe deer at the next turn.

He leaps boulder to boulder, wading the streams,
Foot after foot flows hour after hour.
Relentless, silently, climbing, sneaking,
On the sides of those mountainous towers.

So that day in the mountains closes so quiet
With a meal by the light of the fire.
A man's left with his thoughts as he drifts off to sleep,
The night echoes the blue duck, the town crier.

Now the hills and the weather are sometimes at peace,
But mostly at battle and war.
And the man on the hill is at mercy of both,
Or conquers, grows taller, more sure.

For the worst kind of weather for the hill dwelling man
Is when rain and wind will not let up.
Days turn into weeks, rivers swell, travels stopped,
And the man is entombed in his hut.

So you read every book every page you can find,
Play patience, drink hundreds of brews.
Hopes rise then are dashed when the smallest of gaps
In the weather close, and the torment renews.

I remember the tussock and high country views,
Rugged peaks of cold fingers and fears.
The small huddles of comfort just out of the wind,
Swanny hood protecting my ears.

Wind lashed the tussock, whining and wailing,
Cold cloud would cover the range.

Near vertical spurs disappeared way below,
I'd hobble on in my backyard so strange.

There were nights I recall when the air was so cold
Stewed tea in the billy would freeze.
Nip out of bed quick, the fire would blaze
And a feed and hot brew the cold ease.

So I'd stamp in the snow breathing billows of cloud,
Crunching crisply the crust of the snow.
Splash up the creek, legs numb to the knees
To find where the elusive deer go.

The eyes of the mountain man are never at rest,
Probing deeply, discarding, probing still.
He has a faraway look in his eye
Developed from years on the hill.

Now a deer in the snow covered forest of beech
Is the most beautiful sight you can see.
A paradox occurs, only hunters perceive,
His rifle echoes across the valley.

I remember one evening after a showery day
In tussock north of the Mangaohane,
We spotted a deer on a flat way below,
I went alone, my friend began tea.

Down through drenched bush to the edge of the flat,
His soaked coat fifty paces away.
I edged up to a boulder in the day's dying light,
One shot, by the creek he did lay.

Then a bigger stag broke with a crash from the bush
Crossed the grass at full stride, leaped the stream.
But caught on my crosshair, the rifle did buck,
He rolled into the Toitoi's bright green.

And yet a third from the bush raced out o'er the flat,
Two more shots, he fell dead twice hit.
In seconds three live stags now on that flat lay,
We had venison for tea cooked on a spit.

I smelled a stag on a creek bed late one winter eve
And came across him a few bends further on.
Sneaked through the Pungas till the range was cut short,
Carried him for five hours next morn'.

Having just climbed a waterfall, another evening,
The same creek, deer scent again hit my nose.
It was strong, I froze, eyes piercing, where? there!
She ran, the shot caught her as she rose.

Another evening that winter on a high saddle in thick bush,
Again deer scent came rising and I turned.
Creeping down into the breeze saw deerskin through the leaves,
The echoes rolled, my biggest stag lay in the fern.

Another day I spooked a stag and chased him crashing through the bush,
Running nimbly over obstacles, he was just ahead.
He stopped, I was on a stump, eyes flashed, his antlers moved.
He fell, the bullet took him in the head.

A fern frond flicked behind the upturned roots of a wind felled forest giant.
Only a deer I knew could move it just like that.

Moving right up close I could see his ears six feet away,
I dropped him with rifle high above my hat.

And returning to my car with him firmly on my back
A noise turned me to see an eight pointer just nearby,
Feeding on the leaves of a small tree by the track,
I carried him too, on my back, bye and bye.

Sometimes it seems you cannot go wrong,
You can hit anything you can see.
You don't think, you don't try, just let the shot fly
And the impossible is pulled off with ease.

For the hunter becomes one with his rifle in time
And the rifle becomes one with him.
In his hands all the day to his shoulder it glides
And fires, practiced eyes set the trim.

So years rolled along and memories grew rich,
I remember my first pack wore out.
Rifle blue gone, great dents in my scope,
But the best gear without any doubt.

Oh there's been countless ridges, countless clearings and streams,
Countless struggles and sweat, yes, and tears.
But I wouldn't have missed ought as it's shaped me I know,
A man grew in the midst of those years.

There were others there too in the hills that I met,
Most were visitors, but some belonged.
You see the hills were not made for companies of feet,
Just for few or they hide, they've been wronged.

I remember a dusk at the old Punga Hut
As I leaned on the doorpost by the fire.
A hot mug of tea held tight in both hands,
Soaked socks freshly hung on a wire.

But dry now and warm, the inner man fed well,
A small lamp by the bunk whispering light.
My soul was at peace, I was still, pleasantly tired,
At home on a mid-winter night.

And just before dark as two Moreporks began,
The pungas below damp and calm.
A light fall of snow turned the valley all white
As it painted the pongees drooped arms.

To the right as I stood at the door of the hut
Was a world of cold beauty so clear.
To the left was my fire, billies, sleeping bag, junk!
I'll not forget it the memories so dear.

The master of the domains I had roamed,
A king dressed in back country robes.
No teacher, no guide, self's head walking high,
Every movement and pace, regal pose.

Jesus appeared, He challenged my reign.
The Kings of Kings to a king came.
He humbled His great head and loved me not mine
And I've loved Him, His Kingdom's reclaimed.

No the hills haven't changed where I roamed as a youth,
But I have as horizons have spread.

I've surrendered my life to my Lord Jesus Christ,
I walk now where Jesus did tread.

For when I was young I girded myself
And walked wherever I could.
But now I am older I stretch forth my hands,
He girds me, I walk where He would.

God is my Father. He created my being
As the hills and mountains He made.
And part of His nature expressed in creation
Was built into me when my manhood was laid.